La Tartine Gourmande

LA TARTINE GOURMANDE

Recipes for an Inspired Life

BÉATRICE PELTRE

ROOST
BOOKS

BOSTON · 2011

Roost Books
An imprint of Shambhala Publications, Inc.
Horticultural Hall
300 Massachusetts Avenue
Boston, Massachusetts 02115
roostbooks.com

9 8 7 6 5 4 3 2 1
First Edition
Printed in Singapore

♾ This edition is printed on acid-free paper that meets the
American National Standards Institute z39.48 Standard.
♻ Shambhala Publications makes every effort to print on recycled paper.
For more information please visit www.shambhala.com.
Distributed in the United States by Random House, Inc.,
and in Canada by Random House of Canada Ltd

Design by Greta D. Sibley and Lora Zorian

Library of Congress Cataloging-in-Publication Data

Peltre, Béatrice.
La tartine gourmande: recipes for an inspired life / Béatrice Peltre.—1st ed.
 p.   cm.
Includes index.
ISBN 978-1-59030-762-5 (pbk.: alk. paper)
1. Cooking. 2. Cooking, French. I. Title.
TX714.P4423 2011
641.5944—dc22
2011006799

CONTENTS

ACKNOWLEDGMENTS

When I signed the contract for this cookbook, though I hate to admit it, I panicked. I was nearly four months pregnant with Lulu, our first beautiful baby girl, and I had signed for a dead-line that implied that I was going to cook, write, style, and pho-tograph food while taking care of a newborn. I had no idea what it was going to be like to write a book *and* to be a mother. I hadn't done either before. But somehow, a sweet voice inside was tell-ing me that I could do this, giving me confidence and trust. *Follow your instincts. If it's meant to happen, then it's meant to happen,* it went on. *This is the right time.* I'd been dreaming about a cookbook for many years, mind you, so at least the idea of writing a book wasn't new.

In 2005, I started a Web site called www.beaskitchen.com, in which I collected my favorite recipes. I shared it with friends and family, and anyone asking about a dish they'd enjoyed at my house. The site evolved into www.latartinegourmande.com and a few years later, I find myself here, with this cookbook in my hands. This would never have been possible without the help of the fabulous people I met along the way, people who have constantly encouraged my passion for food and cooking. So I would like to say a heartfelt *merci* to:

Claudia Cross, my agent, for believing in my work and help-ing me through the whole process—from the book proposal to the final contract.

Sara Bercholz, my editor and publisher, who trusted me and gave me this amazing opportunity.

Philip, my husband, for being such a loving supporter of my work, for going grocery shopping at odd times of the evening when I needed a last-minute ingredient, for listening, tasting all the foods, being critical, and pushing me when I *really* needed a push.

Lulu, my beautiful baby daughter, who always put a smile on my face with her giggles, innocence, and *joie de vivre* when I was feeling overwhelmed.

My mother and mother-in-law—aren't mothers the best?—for babysitting Lulu so that I could finish the book and meet my deadline.

My friends and family, for their words of encouragement and for believing in my work.

Sheryl Julian, the *Boston Globe* food editor, who gave me a great opportunity to develop and improve my writing skills, and is such a sweet and a wonderful lady to learn from.

Everyone who tested my recipes and gave me feedback along the way.

The readers of my blog, La Tartine Gourmande, for encouraging me and being my most faithful followers.

What an amazing journey it's been!

THINKING ABOUT FOOD

I am not sure how it all began, this life I have built around food, but I certainly know why. *Chez nous* (at home), thinking about food is a family matter, something running deep in our genes. It seems to have always been this way, occupying a central place in our lives.

Perhaps it started many years ago, when I still lived in the small quiet village of Albestroff *à la campagne* (in the countryside), in northeastern France. I was only a small girl then, mind you, but already rather obsessed with anything food-involved—because to tell the truth, to me, that implied being outdoors too.

There was the obsession I had for my mother's large vegetable garden, *le jardin,* neatly kept at the back of our house; and my aunts' and grandmothers' gardens too. I liked to follow them there on summer afternoons, when it was hot and I could walk barefoot in the grass that felt like straw from the hot sun. Even as a four-year-old I already felt something strong for gardening and getting my hands soiled. I would sit on the dirt-covered path, not far from my aunt Agathe and my cousin Christine, happily petting Minette the stray cat with one hand, and holding a basket tight in the other—ready to help.

"Qu'est-ce que j'peux faire Tata?" ("What can I do, Auntie?") I asked, impatient to get started with a task. It made me feel like a grown-up.

"Y'a des fraises à ramasser, si tu veux" ("There are strawberries to pick"), she shouted back from across the garden as she leaned down, reaching for young French beans.

This was, by far, one of my favorite summer garden activities—because it involved eating the berries while picking. Incidentally, I seemed to be much better at the eating part. French beans, however, were a different matter, and I was glad that *Tata* Agathe never asked that I help with that task. She knew better. If she mentioned green peas, though, I didn't mind. I would settle myself on a wooden stool by the small table tucked under the cherry tree, with one colander between my knees for the pods and another on the table in front of me for the peas. And I set to work, rhythmically: one pea would end up into the colander, the next into my mouth. It seemed to go unnoticed; at least this was what I believed. It's only much later that I learned that no one ever said anything, so as to encourage me to become fond of vegetables. It worked like magic.

At my grandmother's, it was the rabbits and chickens I liked the best. The rabbits because I could pet them; the chickens because they laid eggs. *"Tu me laisseras ramasser les oeufs, dis mémé?"* ("You'll leave the eggs for me to collect, Grandma?") I begged her each time before leaving her house: She was always kind to do so. Every time I walked into her kitchen, my basket filled with dirty feather-covered eggs, I felt like a hunter bringing a treasure home. Also, her *groseilles à maquereaux* (gooseberries) were succulent and juicy, and quite special too, as she was the only one I knew who owned a small bush.

My mother is the one who let me try my hand in the kitchen, and by the age of eight, I was already baking cakes, because anything sweet made more sense to me. I was even allowed to bake alone, following recipes extracted from *Martine fait la cuisine,* a French children's comic strip collection I was addicted to. Martine was my heroine. I wanted to be like her, live her life. Mainly if it meant that I would live in the countryside forever as she did.

There were also the colored notebooks I kept and filled with recipes cut from the French cooking magazines my mother subscribed to. They were all organized by theme: fish, appetizers, vegetables and grains, meat and desserts. The desserts notebook was blue and the thickest. It was also the one I used the most—cakes clearly sounded more interesting than *ratatouille* or *quiche lorraine*.

So there you are. This is how my life with food began. My family educated me in the art of homegrown foods and home-made cooking, and eating well and healthfully. In Albestroff, with a population of barely six hundred—and that's almost counting the cows and sheep—the option of getting takeout did not exist. My mother cooked breakfast, lunch, and din-ner every day. I never questioned it. I just assumed that this was how things were supposed to be. She made a point of cooking according to the seasons and with whatever was available in her garden. I know I was spoiled.

In my family, it's easy to become food obsessed. Everyone con-stantly talks about food. We love to create foods to share. And eat. Many of my friends thought that this all meant that I should become a chef or own a restaurant; it would have made sense, I suppose. I thought about the restaurant idea. For a little while, I even dreamt about running a small place with wooden tables and chairs, decorated with warm colors—a place that would feel like home. I would serve unpretentious soups, savory and sweet tartlets, tasty salads made with rice or quinoa, and sim-ple desserts like chocolate mousse, *île flottantes,* and cherry *cla-foutis*—everything homemade. Somehow, though, I knew that I was not cut out for the job, or those work hours. Instead, I continued to cook for myself and preferred to host dinners for my friends and family. I liked it this way because it meant that I would always have a lovely group of people gathered around an inviting table in the intimacy of my home.

Since then, I have earned degrees in computer science and Eng-

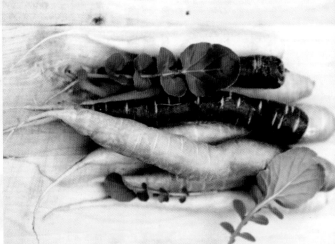

lish; I've traveled the world; lived and worked as a French teacher in New Zealand and as a technical translator in the United States. I married my loving, handsome husband, Philip, with whom I've had Lulu, our adorable baby daughter. It's been a fulfilling life so far.

But during all these years, the people who met me always saw me as the *French girl who travels, cooks, and talks about food all the time*. "Béa thinks about what she's going to cook for dinner or lunch at breakfast," my friend Ron likes to tease. I argue and answer *"Tu exaggères!"* ("You exaggerate!") But you know what? It's true. He is so right! So in November 2005, I decided to start a food blog. "Why not?" I thought. "This is what I like to do, after all." I decided to call my blog "La Tartine Gourmande": *tartine* (an open-faced sandwich commonly eaten in France), because I prepare and eat them so frequently; and *gourmande* (someone who enjoys food), because it defines me well. This blog, I thought, would be a comfortable space where I could freely talk about all the things I like and know well: food and travel.

I never could have imagined what would happen next. To start, that people, many people around the world, would enjoy reading my blabbering about food, and that they'd stop by to write a note and say hello—this was amazing. And then that my life was going to completely change because of it . . .

I am blessed. I am able to do all these things—cook, style, photograph, write, and eat well—and do them for a living. And now, there is this cookbook! Whenever I walk into my kitchen, I am inspired to try new things and prepare more beautiful healthy foods. I want my friends and family to taste and build memories around these foods too. *La Tartine Gourmande: Recipes for an Inspired Life* is all about that. It's about my life and the foods that I like to cook and eat. And it's a warm invitation for you to share in it too.

part one

MY KITCHEN

MY KITCHEN

I should tell you about my kitchen. It's a place at the center
of our house where I spend the largest part of my days, active
behind the stove, with my hands busy chopping, tossing, sauté-
ing, and baking, and where my friends like to hang out when
they visit. It's small—I am still dreaming about that large one,
you know, in the next bigger and better house—but it's warm and
lively because there's always something cooking.

Among my favorite features are a wide spice rack hung above
the gas stove, the purple wood countertop opening into the
kitchen from the dining room, and a tall blackboard that Philip
built for me—it's messy, filled with cooking notes from the
recipes I create, and I like it this way. In the middle, a wooden
kitchen island stands near the stove, with my pots and pans, my
Le Creuset *cocottes* and *tajine* dish, my knives, my mandoline, and
must-have kitchen scale randomly stored underneath.

Like every cook, I have my style; I shape my food with my
soul and the things that matter to me. My cooking naturally
tends to be French (hello *clafoutis, soufflé, crêpes, galettes, mille-feuilles,
papillotes,* and *gratin dauphinois*) because this is who I am and where
I am from, but it is also largely influenced by my travels around
the world. Reading through these pages, you'll see that cooking

healthfully is a priority, and so is the use of fresh seasonal produce. I draw my cooking creativity from the people I meet and the food markets and places I visit. You'll find a wide palette of vegetable dishes that show my great fondness for vegetables, fresh herbs, and fruit, reminding me of the gardens my family keeps in France; risottos and pasta dishes that are inspired from my trips to Italy; *tartines* and seasonal soups that are what we regularly eat for lunch or dinner because that's what my mother taught me to do; sweet and savory tarts that draw me close to my French roots; rustic and elegant desserts because a meal without dessert is like wearing only one shoe. *Non?* You get the gist of it.

GUIDELINES

These two simple tips will ensure that any recipe you make will come out beautifully.

Number one: Always read a recipe in full before you start cooking. Once that's done, gather the ingredients and utensils that you'll need. I learned these tips from my mother, and any cook worth her cake will tell you the same. This will also make the whole cooking process easier and much more enjoyable.

Number two: Weigh the ingredients if you can, especially when baking. Measuring with cups isn't often precise. For example, 1 cup of chopped chocolate can vary greatly in weight depending on how big the chunks are. A kitchen scale is an extremely useful tool; you may want to consider purchasing one if you haven't already.

MY INGREDIENTS

Let's start with the sweet matter: baking. You'll notice that most of the flours I use in my recipes are gluten-free. It's a deliberate choice, not a medical one. A few years ago I was told that I should avoid gluten for a short time (I do not have celiac disease, but have a predisposition to gluten intolerance). I'm sure you can imagine my first reaction and my concern too. I remember asking *"Quoi?"* ("What?") *"Really?"* and shaking my head to make it go away. Tears and discouragement followed. After all, what is a French woman to do without baguette and *pain au chocolat*? Once I had calmed down, though, I thought, "OK, I can do this, I'm willing to give it a try."

So one day, I drove to the market to purchase quinoa, amaranth, buckwheat, hazelnut, and millet flours, in place of the wheat flours I was more familiar with. The many types of flours I found impressed me. During the weeks that followed, I started to experiment. I'd weigh and mix flours, adding a bit of this and a bit of that, waiting to see what would happen. I felt like a chemist in her laboratory, watching experiments develop in front of my eyes. *It's exciting,* I'd think, my hands covered with flour, *I wonder what I'm going to end up with*. Will the cake rise? What about the muffins? What will they taste like? I baked cakes, muffins, cookies, brownies, ladyfingers, and crusts to make savory and sweet tarts.

The first cakes looked funny, and the crusts fell apart. But I wasn't ready to give up. And sure enough, at some point along the way, things started to improve and taste really good. *I like this,* I thought. "This muffin is so tasty!" Philip said, one day, after swallowing a piece of a chocolate apple hazelnut cake I'd just taken out of the oven—a sure sign of success. My muffins were moist, the cakes were rich; the tarts were light and flavorful. It was all so yummy that I was converted and decided to make gluten-free flours the standard in my pantry. In the end, this shift was a blessing because not only did I improve my baking skills, but since these flours have better nutritional values than most wheat flours, the foods I now make are even more healthy.

Flours

Here is a selection of the flours I like to use—always organic, whenever I can, just like most of the produce I buy—they are the ones you'll find in this book. You can feel free to substitute wheat flours, if you prefer. Note, though, that the taste will be different, as the recipes have been tested with the ingredients indicated. I highly suggest refrigerating flours in containers, as it increases their shelf life.

- **Quinoa flour** is produced from the South American grain-like seed quinoa. Quinoa is rich in protein and nutrients, especially amino acids. It's a flour that gives character to baked goods and makes them deliciously moist. I rarely use quinoa flour alone but prefer to combine it with other flours, such as amaranth, millet, or rice flours.
- **Quinoa flakes** are produced from steam-rolled quinoa. They are quick to cook and impart a nice lightness to whatever you cook with them: muffins, cakes, cookies. They are also excellent in pancakes or waffles. Another idea is to use them in place of oatmeal for a nutritious breakfast.
- **White rice flour** is milder, lighter, and easier to digest than

wheat flour. It is also grainier, making it a flour that is best combined with other flours.

- **Brown rice flour** is similar to white rice flour in texture but has higher nutritional values—it's rich in vitamin E and iron, among other nutrients. Like white rice flour, it's best combined with other flours.

- **Amaranth flour** is high in fiber, calcium, and iron. It has a relatively high concentration of vitamins like magnesium, phosphorus, copper, and manganese, and a nearly complete set of amino acids, which you won't find in many other grains. Like white and brown rice flours, it's best if it's used with other flours. It has a mild but distinct sweet, nutty, and maltlike flavor; I find that it works really well with chocolate.

- **Sweet rice flour,** also known as Mochiko flour, is made from mochi rice, a sticky and glutinous rice popular in many Asian countries. Mochiko flour is rather starchy, and works well in baked goods such as muffins, pancakes, waffles, or cookies, as it binds ingredients together. It imparts a light taste and more delicate texture than wheat flour.

- **Buckwheat flour** is a wonderful flour to work with: It has a rich, earthy flavor and a very high nutritional value. In spite of its name, buckwheat is not a type of wheat, but is actually an herb plant related to rhubarb. It is rich in protein, manganese, magnesium, and fiber. In France, it is commonly used in the preparation of savory *crêpes* called *"galettes."* I like to use it when I make *blini* or bake muffins and cakes, especially when chocolate is involved.

- **Millet flour** is derived from the millet grain, which is popular in Africa and India, and is also one of the most popular grains in the world. Millet is related to sorghum and is also highly nutritious and extremely easy to digest.

- **Xanthan gum** is produced by fermentation of glucose or sucrose and is often used in gluten-free baking for adding viscosity. I use it particularly when I make crusts; it will make them less crumbly, as it replaces the missing gluten, so to speak.

- **Almond flour** is wonderful in cakes and sweet crusts, adding grittiness to the texture. It is high in protein, manganese, potassium, and vitamin E, and contains healthy

monounsaturated fats. It is fairly mild in taste. You can buy
it or make it yourself by grinding whole blanched almonds
into a fine powder in a food processor. Be careful not to
grind the almonds too much, though, otherwise you might
end up with almond butter. If you decide to make your own,
it's best to use small quantities at a time, and use the pulse
option of your food processor. You can also find and use
almond meal, which is similar to almond flour (except that
the almonds used have the skin on). I typically use them
interchangeably.

· **Hazelnut flour,** like other nut flours, makes baked goods
moist. It is low in carbohydrates and is a good source of
dietary fiber and protein. The flour is sweet in flavor, with
a slightly more pronounced nutty taste than almond flour.
You can buy this flour or, like with almond flour, make it
yourself. Toasting the flour before using it also gives it more
body, emphasizing its nutty flavor.

Many of the flours listed can be purchased at natural foods
stores, such as Whole Foods, as well as at some major grocery
stores. They are also available online. Some of my favorite Web
sites are www.bobsredmill.com and www.glutenfreemall.com.

Oils and Vinegars

"Dis-donc, tu en as des huiles et des vinaigres!" ("Well, you surely have
quite a selection of oils and vinegars!") my mother exclaimed
when she opened my kitchen cabinet. It's full of bottles of all
shapes and colors, filled with olive, vegetable, and nut oils, and
vinegars—stored in no particular order. She had to comment
on that too. And smiled.

"Tu crois?" ("Do you think so?") I responded. "Well, you
know, it's like a dress or a pair of shoes, you need the matching
bag to go along, right?" So I like to keep a wide selection of oils
and vinegars handy, using them to pair with the foods I decide
to cook.

Olive oils, for example: I use some for cooking and sauté-
ing, and others, typically the more expensive ones, to prepare

vinaigrettes. I am a lover of nuts, so I have a lot of different nut oils (these I prefer to store in the fridge for longer shelf life), such as pecan, hazelnut, walnut, almond, avocado, and pistachio, each with its own particular flavor. For vinegars, you'll see that I keep a wide selection too, with rice, apple cider, white and red wine, balsamic, sherry, and Banyuls vinegars (a French sweet wine vinegar with delicate aromas of hazelnut and berries) to complement each particular dish.

Chocolate

During the many months of writing this cookbook, there was always a bar of dark chocolate next to my keyboard. When my head felt blurry, I would take a piece and stuff it in my mouth. The truth is that there is always a supply of chocolate at home, or in my handbag—ask my friends—to eat or for me to bake with. I like dark chocolate with 64% or more cocoa content. When I bake, I use the French brand Valrhona, by far my favorite, and this is what I've used in all the chocolate recipes you'll find in this book. But of course, you can use what you like best. Here are a few guidelines about the different Valrhona chocolates I used:

> Gianduja noisette: The chocolate I refer to as "hazelnut-flavored chocolate"
> Manjari: The chocolate I refer to as "dark chocolate with 64% cocoa contents"
> Guanaja: The chocolate I refer to as "dark chocolate with 70% cocoa contents"
> Milk chocolate: The chocolate I refer to as "chocolate with 40% cocoa contents"
> And white chocolate

Gelatin

I use gelatin sheets instead of gelatin powder; this is how it's commonly sold in France—I had actually never seen gelatin powder before moving to the United States—so it's what I'm used to. Therefore, you'll see that my recipes call for gelatin sheets and are tested with them. If you prefer gelatin powder, that's fine too. The conversion goes as follows (keep in mind that the strength of gelatin varies from brand to brand, so it's a good idea to test and once you're happy with the texture, use the ratio you feel comfortable with): 1 gelatin sheet (2 g; .07 oz) = ¾ teaspoon gelatin powder. It's useful to know that 1 envelope Knox = 7 g; .25 oz = 3 teaspoons = 1 tablespoon = 4 gelatin sheets. If you prefer to use gelatin powder, follow the instructions on the package. Generally, you will need to sprinkle the gelatin powder over a cold liquid and let it bloom for 1 minute before adding it to a warm preparation so that it dissolves completely. For example, when using 2 teaspoons gelatin powder, use 2 ½ tablespoons cold water.

Sugars

- **Blond cane sugar** is also called "unrefined sugar," "cane sugar," or "crystallized cane juice." For substitution, use regular white sugar.
- **Muscovado sugar** has a fine, moist texture with a subtle taste of molasses. There are two types, light and dark. It can be substituted with light or dark brown sugar if you cannot find muscovado sugar. Store it in an airtight container.

MY EQUIPMENT

Quand on veut on peut. (Where there's a will, there's a way.)

If you like to cook, you can do it pretty much anywhere, with anything handy. Don't you think so?

In the winter of 2003, Philip and I spent a week on Hook Island in the Whitsundays, one of those pretty islands off the eastern coast of Australia. It was hot and sunny—since it was summer in the Southern Hemisphere—which was a welcoming change from the freezing cold weather back home in wintry Boston! We were traveling for five weeks and decided to take a break from our busy itinerary, to relax, snorkel, hike, read, and cook simple foods. I had found a cheap backpackers' place to stay—the only place we could afford at that time.

We didn't have much to cook with. Hook Island is rugged with very few inhabitants, so there was hardly any food to buy, besides rum, vanilla ice cream cones, bags of spicy chips, pizza, and a few other foods *so* unappealing that, I am convinced, I intentionally erased them from my memory. Normally, I would have panicked at the thought of not having fresh foods to cook with, but I had planned ahead with a few bags of groceries purchased in Mackay on the way to the ferry. Philip hadn't wanted to stop at the grocery store, but I remember thinking it would be a bad idea not to. "I am sure we'll find something there," he said confidently. "We don't need more stuff!" But the words "island," "small," and "not even a road" kept resonating in my head. *Hint, hint!* In the end, we were glad to arrive with our groceries, even if it was a lot to carry.

Each night I would take my ingredients out of the communal fridge and start to cook. Other guests, I noticed, kept eyeing me while they were preparing their meal at the other end of the table, with a *where-did-you-find-that* kind of look on their faces. I would have shared, but our supplies had to feed us for breakfast, lunch, and dinner for the entire week!

The kitchen was extremely basic. There were a few pots, a scratched frying pan, mismatched plates and forks, and a few mugs. When I was lucky, I'd put my hand on the only decent knife before anyone else grabbed it. *This will do,* I'd tell myself, feeling both challenged and confident.

I cooked simple, unpretentious dinners. One night, we had a zucchini and carrot stew cooked with onions, garlic, and freshly chopped parsley—a meal my mother often prepared at home. We ate it with jasmine rice and a tossed salad on the side. Another night, it was a dish of spaghetti dressed with cherry tomatoes, lemon, crushed garlic, and thyme. When dinner was ready, we'd sit in front of our cabin and eat, watching the sunset with our feet dipped into the turquoise-hued water.

Life felt pretty good.

"Our trip pushed my limits," I told Philip one night after we'd returned to Boston.

"What do you mean?" he asked without paying much attention to what I was saying.

"Well, I don't need much to cook with." That had him stop what he was doing right away.

"Really?" he said, cheeringly. "Good! That means you don't need to buy more stuff!"

I smiled; he did too. He knew me better.

Though I may not need much, given the choice, I like a well-equipped kitchen. We all do, *non*? There are some things, call them gadgets if you like, that can make the life of a cook—you, me—much more comfortable and happy. Here's a list of special equipment that I like to have on hand. With these things you will be well prepared to make everything in this book, with a smile on your face to boot.

- **A kitchen scale**: Weighing ingredients is much more reliable than measuring them with cups. Even more so when you bake. I keep two scales, an electronic one that I received as a gift, and a mechanical one—cheap, green, and really cute on the countertop—that do the job.

- **A mandoline**: I can't begin to tell you how much I like my mandoline—and how much I wouldn't do without one. It gives such better results when you want to slice vegetables paper-thin, like a bulb of fennel or a radish. You don't need a professional mandoline, mind you. In fact, the inexpensive ones easily found at Asian markets are my favorite. Benriner makes a great Japanese mandoline, and this is the one I use.

- **A juicer**: Once you've tasted a freshly squeezed apple juice versus one that is bottled, it's really difficult to not always want *that exact same freshly squeezed apple juice* every day. It's so delicious, and so healthy! Hence the reason why, one day, I decided to invest in the purchase of a juicer, which I leave on my countertop—and I never regretted my purchase. Besides using the juicer in some of my recipes, I also use it to prepare fresh vegetable and fruit juices, like apple and carrot, that we enjoy at different moments of the day.

- **A food processor**: This kitchen appliance makes many preparation steps much easier and faster. With it, you can grate vegetables, blend soups, and grind nuts in a snap.

- **A stand mixer**: This is the kitchen appliance that I literally use every time I bake: It's sturdy, quick, stable, and strong. I use it to beat egg whites, beat eggs with sugar, cream butter with sugar, and prepare bread and pie crust. Mine is a cheery orange KitchenAid and has become indispensable. If you don't own one, use a hand mixer instead.

- **A spice grinder (or a coffee grinder)**: I find this appliance extremely useful if, for example, I need to grind lemongrass finely. It's also great for grinding small amounts of nuts. It's not completely necessary but nice to have.

- **Tart and tartlet molds**: I prefer to use molds with removable bottoms, as they make it easier to unmold baked goods.

The standard sizes I keep are 4 ½-inch molds for tartlets, and 9- and 10-inch molds for larger tarts.

- **Ring molds:** These are mostly used for special-occasion cakes. For individual cakes I use 2 ¾-inch-wide by 2 ¼-inch-tall ring molds (I own a set of six, for convenience). I also keep a set of 4-inch-wide by 1 ¾-inch-tall ring molds handy, ideal for a crust without a rim, or to plate a pretty appetizer, such as a fish *ceviche*. Then, I have an adjustable 7-inch-wide by 2 ¾-inch-tall ring mold, perfect to make cakes like a fruit *charlotte* or a layered chocolate mousse.

- **Plastic cake wraps:** These are liners I use inside a ring mold when I prepare special-occasion cakes. They can be purchased in kitchen specialty stores and come in sheets or large rolls, in different sizes. Mine fit 2 ¾-inch-tall ring molds.

MY BASIC RECIPES
AND METHODS

BASIC RECIPES

You will find these recipes called for throughout this book.
The tart crusts are gluten free because I find gluten-free
flours—such as millet, quinoa, amaranth, or buckwheat—more
flavorful. Incidentally, they are also more nutritious. These
tart crusts, however, can also be made with wheat flours, though
proportions may need adjusting, as the weight of the different
flours may vary.

    The tart crusts that follow can be frozen. Wrap tightly in
plastic wrap before freezing. When you want to use it, place
the crust in the fridge the night before. If you are planning on
making tartlets—which you'll see is something I always favor
because I am a lover of individual servings—I suggest dividing
the crust before refrigerating or freezing it; this way it will be
ready to be rolled. Note that although the book suggests making
the crusts with a stand mixer or food processor, they can all be
made by hand—the way my mother taught me.

A note about rolling a crust, especially if it's made using gluten-free flours. Start by cleaning a wide area on the kitchen countertop. Flour it generously. Flour your hands and rolling pin too. When making a gluten-free crust, since there isn't any gluten (what keeps the ingredients together and makes the crust elastic), working the crust might seem more challenging. Just go slow. If the crust breaks in some parts when you roll it, don't worry. Place it in the mold and patch the rough areas, pressing gently with the tips of your fingers, the way you would if you only pressed the dough to garnish a mold. It will not affect the end result by any means. For best results, you can add xanthan gum to the dry ingredients, as suggested in the recipes in this book. This allows for the crust to have more elasticity and be rolled easily. Also, when making a crust, sometimes you might end up with a tiny bit left over. What I like to do is to freeze the leftovers, well labeled so I can remember what they are and when I made them, for future use. Or I refrigerate the leftovers wrapped in plastic wrap, and use within two to three days. This way, I can easily improvise a quick savory tart or dessert.

For each tart, if you make the larger version, there will be leftover dough.

Pâte sucrée (Sweet crust)

To be prepared 3 hours ahead, or the day before.

In the bowl of a stand mixer fitted with the paddle blade, combine the flours, cornstarch, xanthan gum, and confectioners' sugar. Work on medium speed to obtain a fine mixture. Add the butter and work again until crumbles form. Add the egg and work until the dough detaches from the bowl and forms a ball. Wrap in plastic wrap and refrigerate for a minimum of 3 hours. Bring to room temperature before using (about 30 minutes, when the crust doesn't feel hard).

Makes four 4 ½-inch tartlets or one 10-inch tart

⅓ cup (60 g; 2 oz) white rice flour
⅓ cup (40 g; 1 ½ oz) quinoa flour
⅓ cup (40 g; 1 ½ oz) cornstarch
1 ½ teaspoons xanthan gum
⅓ cup (40 g; 1 ½ oz) confectioners' sugar
7 tablespoons (100 g; 3 ½ oz), unsalted butter, chilled and diced
1 small egg

Lemon-flavored olive oil crust

In the bowl of a food processor fitted with the dough blade, combine the millet, quinoa, and brown rice flours with the almond meal, xanthan gum, sugar, and lemon zest and pulse to combine. Add the olive oil and egg, and process until all the ingredients are combined, scraping the sides of the bowl as you go. Add the water, 1 tablespoon at a time, and work until the crust forms a ball. Do not work it too much. At this point, divide the crust into 4 smaller balls so it is easier to roll. Generously flour a working surface as well as your hands and a rolling pin. Roll the dough into rounds the size of your tartlet or tart mold(s). Refrigerate the crust, covered with parchment paper, for 30 minutes.

Makes four 4 ½-inch tartlets or one 10-inch tart

⅔ cup (80 g; 2 ¾ oz) millet flour
⅓ cup (40 g; 1 ½ oz) quinoa flour
⅓ cup (60 g; 2 oz) white (or brown) rice flour
⅓ cup (40 g; 1 ½ oz) almond meal
1 ½ teaspoons xanthan gum
2 tablespoons (20 g; ¾ oz) blond cane sugar
Finely grated zest of 1 small lemon
¼ cup (60 ml) olive oil
1 small egg, lightly beaten with a fork
4 to 5 tablespoons cold water (If you use a large egg, reduce the amount of water to 2 to 3 tablespoons.)

Rustic vanilla and amaranth sweet crust

Makes four 4 ½-inch tartlets or one 10-inch tart

⅓ cup (50 g; 1 ¾ oz) amaranth flour
⅓ cup (40 g; 1 ½ oz) millet flour
⅓ cup (30 g; 1 oz) quinoa flakes
⅓ cup (40 g; 1 ½ oz) cornstarch
1 ½ teaspoons xanthan gum
1 vanilla bean, split open and seeds
    scraped out
2 tablespoons blond cane sugar
Pinch of sea salt
6 tablespoons (85 g; 3 oz) unsalted
    butter, chilled and diced
1 small egg
2 to 3 tablespoons cold water

To be prepared 1 hour ahead, or the day before.

In the bowl of a stand mixer fitted with the paddle blade, combine the flours, quinoa flakes, cornstarch, xanthan gum, vanilla seeds, sugar, and sea salt. Add the butter and beat on medium speed until crumbles form. Add the egg and continue to beat until incorporated. Gradually add the water while beating until the dough detaches from the bowl and forms a ball. If using for tartlets, divide the dough into 6 smaller balls (one for each tartlet) and wrap in plastic wrap. Refrigerate for a minimum of 1 hour before using. If it's in the fridge for a few hours or overnight, take out of the fridge at least 30 minutes before using.

Brown rice, quinoa, and buckwheat crust

Makes six 4 ½-inch tartlets or one 12-inch tart

½ cup (90 g; 3 oz) brown rice flour
    or white rice flour
⅓ cup (50 g; 1 ¾ oz) buckwheat flour
⅓ cup (40 g; 1 ½ oz) quinoa flour
1 ½ teaspoons xanthan gum
½ teaspoon sea salt
1 tablespoon poppy seeds (optional)
6 tablespoons (85 g; 3 oz) unsalted
    butter, chilled and diced
1 small egg
3 tablespoons cold water

To be prepared 1 hour ahead, or the day before.

In the bowl of a stand mixer fitted with the paddle blade, combine the flours, xanthan gum, sea salt, and poppy seeds (if using). Add the butter and beat on medium speed until crumbles form. Add the egg and continue to beat until incorporated. Gradually add the water while beating until the dough detaches from the bowl and forms a ball. If using for tartlets, divide the dough into 6 smaller balls (one for each tartlet) and wrap in plastic wrap. Refrigerate for a minimum of 1 hour before using. If it's in the fridge for a few hours or overnight, take out of the fridge at least 30 minutes before using.

Millet, amaranth, and brown rice crust

To be prepared 1 hour ahead, or the day before.

In the bowl of a stand mixer fitted with the paddle blade, combine the flours, xanthan gum, and sea salt. Add the butter and beat on medium speed until crumbles form. Add the egg and continue to beat until incorporated. Gradually add the water while beating until the dough detaches from the bowl and forms a ball. If using for tartlets, divide the dough into 6 smaller balls (one for each tartlet) and wrap in plastic wrap. Refrigerate for a minimum of 1 hour before using. If it's in the fridge for a few hours or overnight, take out of the fridge at least 30 minutes before using.

Makes six 4 ½-inch tartlets or one 12-inch tart

⅔ cup (80 g; 2 ¾ oz) millet flour

⅓ cup (50 g; 1 ¾ oz) amaranth flour

⅓ cup (60 g; 1 ½ oz) brown rice flour

1 ½ teaspoons xanthan gum

½ teaspoon sea salt

7 tablespoons (100 g; 3 ½ oz) unsalted butter, chilled and diced

1 small egg

3 tablespoons cold water, or more if needed

Sweet rice, quinoa, and amaranth crust

To be prepared 1 hour ahead, or the day before.

In the bowl of a stand mixer fitted with the paddle blade, combine the flours, xanthan gum, and sea salt. Add the butter and mix on medium speed until crumbles form. Add the egg and mix again. Add the water gradually and continue mixing until the dough detaches from the bowl and forms a ball. Wrap in plastic wrap and refrigerate for a minimum of 1 hour before using. If it's in the fridge for a few hours or overnight, take out of the fridge at least 30 minutes before using.

Makes six 4 ½-inch tartlets or one 12-inch tart

½ cup (80 g; 2 ¾ oz) sweet rice flour

½ cup (60 g; 2 oz) quinoa flour

½ cup (70 g; 2 ½ oz) amaranth flour

1 ½ teaspoons xanthan gum

½ teaspoon sea salt

7 tablespoons (100 g; 3 ½ oz) unsalted butter, chilled and diced

1 small egg

4 tablespoons cold water, or more if needed

Ladyfingers

Makes eighteen to twenty 3-inch ladyfingers

You will need: a pastry bag
fitted with a ¾-inch opening

3 tablespoons (30 g; 1 oz) white rice
flour
3 tablespoons (30 g; 1 oz)
quinoa flour
⅓ cup (40 g; 1 ½ oz) cornstarch
3 large eggs, separated
Pinch of sea salt
⅓ cup (75 g; 2 ½ oz) blond cane
sugar
3 to 4 heaping teaspoons confectioners' sugar, for dusting

Preheat the oven to 350°F (180°C). Cover 2 baking sheets with parchment paper; set aside.

In a bowl, sift the flours and cornstarch; set aside. In the bowl of a stand mixer fitted with the whisk, beat the egg whites with the sea salt. When they form soft peaks, add 1 tablespoon of the sugar and continue to beat. Progressively add the rest of the sugar until stiff peaks form. Continue beating and add the egg yolks.

Using a spatula, gently fold the flour mixture into the egg batter, making sure to keep it airy. Using a pastry bag fitted with a ¾-inch opening, pipe 2 ½-inch-long sticks onto your parchment-lined baking sheets, with about 1 inch of space between them (they will spread a little while baking). Dust with confectioners' sugar and let rest for a minute until the sugar is absorbed, then repeat a second time.

Place the ladyfingers in the oven and bake for 14 to 15 minutes, until they are lightly golden. With a spatula, carefully transfer them to a cooling rack and leave to cool completely. The ladyfingers keep for a week in an airtight container.

Homemade vegetable broth

In a large stockpot, heat the oil over medium heat. Add the coriander and fennel seeds, thyme, and peppercorns. Cook for about 1 minute, until fragrant. Add the onion and garlic and continue to cook for 2 minutes, without browning. Add the rest of the vegetables, salt, and bay leaf and cook for 10 minutes, stirring occasionally. Add the water, bring to a boil, then reduce the heat and simmer, covered, for 20 minutes.

Remove from the heat, add the parsley, and let the broth sit for a few hours, covered, or refrigerate overnight for the flavors to develop. Strain the broth and use as needed. At this point, you can keep it for 3 to 4 days in the fridge or strain and freeze it for up to 1 month.

Makes 5 ½ cups

2 tablespoons olive oil

¼ teaspoon coriander seeds

¼ teaspoon fennel seeds

3 fresh thyme twigs

5 peppercorns

1 yellow onion, finely chopped

3 garlic cloves, minced

1 leek, white part only, diced

1 fennel bulb, with greens attached, coarsely chopped

3 carrots, peeled and diced

2 celery stalks, diced

1 bay leaf

1 teaspoon sea salt

6 cups (1 liter 420 ml) cold water

2 tablespoons coarsely chopped flat-leaf parsley

Crème anglaise à la vanille (Vanilla-flavored custard)

Makes 1 ⅓ cups

1 cup (235 ml) whole milk

1 vanilla bean, split open and seeds
   scraped out

3 large egg yolks

2 tablespoons blond cane sugar

Use a *crème anglaise* to accompany a chocolate cake, an apple tart, *crêpes,* or bread pudding; or simply eat it with fresh, juicy berries. It's always divine, even when you eat it plain with a spoon.

Note: You can substitute other spices such as cardamom, cinnamon, or star anise, or a combination of a few for the vanilla.

In a pot, combine the milk and the vanilla bean and seeds and bring to a boil over medium heat (check that it does not overflow). When it reaches the boiling point, remove from the heat, cover, and let infuse for 30 minutes to 1 hour. Using a fine sieve or *chinois,* strain the milk and discard the vanilla bean. Keep warm over low heat.

Meanwhile, in a bowl, beat the egg yolks with the sugar until light and pale in color. Pour in the milk slowly while stirring continuously. Transfer the custard back to the pot and cook over medium-low heat, stirring constantly, until the cream thickens—it should never boil. The custard is ready when it coats a spoon—this takes from 7 to 10 minutes, depending on the heat of your stove. Once the custard is ready, transfer to a bowl and let cool, stirring occasionally.

Cover with plastic wrap and refrigerate until ready to use. The custard keeps for 2 to 3 days in the fridge.

If you'd like the custard to be a little thicker, add 1 teaspoon cornstarch after beating the egg yolks with the sugar, and proceed in the same way for the next steps. A traditional *crème anglaise,* the way I learned to make it, does not use cornstarch. However, it is an ingredient you may like to add in order to obtain a thicker custard. Try both and see what you like best.

Reusing vanilla beans: Once you've cooked with a vanilla bean, wash it under cold water and dry it. Place the bean in a jar filled with sugar. This is the easiest way to make homemade vanilla-flavored sugar. It works wonderfully.

BASIC COOKING TECHNIQUES

These are simple cooking techniques used throughout the book. Refer to them when they are mentioned in a recipe.

Prebake a Crust (Blind Baking)

This is the process of cooking a tart crust before adding the topping. Once you have rolled out the dough and pressed it into the tart mold, cover it with a piece of parchment paper, and top it with pie weights (dry rice or beans work too). Bake the crust for 10 to 15 minutes, typically at 350°F (180°C) or at the temperature indicated in the recipe. Sometimes, if the recipe calls for it, you'll bake the crust for an extra 5 minutes without the parchment paper and weights.

Bain-Marie

This is the process by which you melt or heat ingredients by putting them in a bowl that is then placed over a pot of simmering water. Make sure that the bowl never touches the water. This method is often used to melt chocolate and butter.

Water Bath

This method uses a pan of water placed in an oven—the hot water provides a constant, steady heat source and ensures even, slow cooking. Place the dishes containing the food into a larger pan. Place the pan in the oven, then add enough hot water to the pan so that it reaches halfway up the dishes containing the food. Take care that the water doesn't spill into the food when you remove the dishes and pan from the oven.

Blanch Vegetables

This is the process by which you precook vegetables for a short period of time in a large volume of salted boiling water. If you want to keep the vegetables crunchy and green—asparagus, French beans, or peas, for example—it's important to keep the cooking time short. Rinse the vegetables under cold to iced water once they are cooked.

part two

THE RECIPES

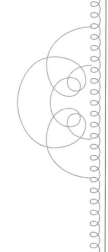

Breakfast and Brunch to Inspire

I heard my stomach grumble. *"J'ai faim!"* ("I am hungry!") I
whispered softly in Philip's ear as we were lying in bed, with
Lulu cozily nested between us. It was only 6:00 a.m., but we
were awake. Our sweet baby daughter was playing with her feet,
grabbing one with each hand before stuffing them into her
mouth, like a greedy lioness. She turned her head to her right,
then her left, and then she smiled when she saw that her *papa*
and *maman* were looking back at her, smiling too, despite the
early hour.

"I know! I can tell you're hungry," Philip answered with a
big yawn stretching his face. My stomach was making obvious
loud noises. "See! Lulu is noticing too," he added when she
looked at me, hearing more noise coming from my stomach.

"*Really,* I am! I have to get up!" I insisted.

I am a breakfast person—I always have been. I invariably
wake up in the morning excited about setting the table and
starting the day with food. *Oh,* food! It's funny in a way because
I don't come from a food culture where breakfast or brunch is a
priority. In France, we have *croissants* and *pains au chocolat* and *pains
aux raisins,* but frankly, these are not the foods that I am excited
about in the morning. Perhaps because I find them too rich for
my morning taste buds.

When I was twelve, I flew on an airplane for the first time and traveled to London, England. I remember how nervous and excited I was. It was my *first* trip alone, and it was my *first* trip to an English-speaking country where people speak "a funny language," as my Dad always likes to say. "Hello" and "thanks" (he pronounces it "tanks," with an impressively strong French accent) are the extent of his grasp of the language, but he still has to have a strong opinion about it—that's my dad.

I was going to visit Liz, my English pen pal. She and I only knew each other through the few letters we had exchanged, hers in broken French, and mine in broken English, but that did not stop us from becoming best friends. Liz was funny and lively. She looked very English to me with her beautiful curly red hair and big teeth that filled her entire mouth. Her mother, Kate, was sweet like a pie. She always spoke in a very soft voice, which incidentally made it hard for me to understand her. So we spent a lot of time just smiling at each other, and that was good enough. We realized that we didn't really need words when it came to food. Especially when she'd make apple pie for dessert—I still haven't eaten a better one since then.

One night, she talked about making a *crumble*. "What is that?" I asked, intrigued. "It's an English dessert for you to try," she replied with a generous smile lighting her pretty face. It was hard for me to imagine that something could be better than her apple pie. But by late afternoon, when the aroma of baked fruit and sugar started to fill the air in the house, so sweet and intoxicating, I sensed that whatever she had been baking in the minuscule oven in her tiny kitchen was probably going to be amazing. She prepared the dessert with a crusty whole-wheat topping made with rolled oats and nuts, and young rhubarb as the fruit. It was almost too warm to eat when she brought it to the table, but no one was ready to wait. *"Ouah!"* I exclaimed after the first taste, unable to refrain from making noises that expressed my delight. "That's really good!" It was actually beyond delicious.

Kate made homemade and organic a priority—a way of life. For breakfast, we'd start the day with granola she'd prepared for the week, eaten with plain yogurt—and tea. *Oh the tea!* I had never drunk tea or eaten granola before. Scrambled eggs with toast and orange marmalade often followed. Every bite tasted delicious and new.

One day, we had brunch in a nearby pub. *Brunch!* Talk about a new food adventure, for a French girl too! The pub smelled of beer and cigarettes, two things that, under most circumstances, would have put me off. But this time I was too interested in my food to care: We had jacket potatoes with prawns, island sauce, and pickles, with a Bibb salad on the side. I remember scooping out the buttery flesh of the potato, savoring each bite to prolong the moment. I wanted it to last forever.

When I returned home to France, I raved about how wonderful the food in England was. Everyone in the family looked at me with dubious smiles, before adding *"Vraiment?"* ("Really?")—particularly my dad. I didn't care. I was determined to cook English food for them. So I made apple crumbles and granolas. I prepared sweet cucumber pickles, crisp jacket potatoes, and scrambled eggs. And everyone, even my dad, ate and enjoyed the foods I brought to the table. I knew they would.

I became fascinated by breakfast and brunch. And now, in every country I visit, I always ask the people we meet about their breakfast habits.

In Nova Scotia, where Philip and I traveled once, it was Bob's pancakes that piqued my curiosity. We were staying at a charming B&B by the water near the Cabot Trail. Bob was the owner of the B&B. He was a tall man in his mid-sixties, and although he looked imposing, he made us feel at home right away—especially with his pancakes. Every morning, he served them with a generous amount of local maple syrup and a tall glass of apple juice that, he was proud to tell us, he'd made himself. The pancakes smelled of sugar and sweet butter, filling the plate like puffed jewels in a golden sea. I was taken by the taste right away.

Sometimes the most innocent thought of food wakes me up in the middle of the night because I am dreaming that I'm eating. I know, this is hard to believe, but it's so true. Though I don't always remember what I'm eating in the dream, I know it must be tasty, as my mouth waters and my stomach grumbles, so much so that I wake up.

So I don't fight it. I get up, eager to start the day with two of my favorite activities: making and eating food.

Fresh muesli
with yogurt, raspberries, apples, and nuts

Philip likes porridge a lot. Everyone in his Irish family does. Before I met him, I had never eaten it. I remember the first time I ate it and how much I enjoyed the soft texture of the warm cereal in my mouth. For two entire weeks, I begged that he make it every morning for us. When I first moved in with him, Philip encouraged me to use oats more. One thing led to another, and I was inspired to create this muesli—one of our favorites for breakfast. It's a fresh and utterly delicious recipe—food that is a perfect way to start the day. Feel free to substitute fruits that are in season, such as blueberries, black currants, or even cranberries.

Serves 4

2 cups (200 g; 7 oz) quick-cooking rolled oats
2 cups apple juice
2 cups (250 g; 8 ¾ oz) fresh raspberries
2 tablespoons blond cane sugar
6 tablespoons slivered almonds
1 large apple, such as a pink lady or a local heirloom variety
Lime or lemon juice, to taste
Whole plain yogurt, to taste
2 tablespoons shelled unsalted green pistachios, chopped
Maple syrup or honey, to serve

Start the night before.

In a bowl, pour the apple juice over the oats to cover. Let the oats sit overnight, covered, in the fridge.

The next day, combine the raspberries and sugar in a small pot. Place over medium heat and cook until the raspberries become soft, about 4 minutes; remove from the heat and let cool.

Toast the almonds in a frying pan for 4 or 5 minutes, until lightly brown and fragrant; remove from the heat and set aside to cool.

Grate the apple and squeeze lime juice on top to prevent discoloration.

Divide the oats among 4 bowls. Add the apple, raspberry purée, yogurt, pistachios, and almonds to each bowl. Top with a drizzle of maple syrup or honey and a squeeze of lime or lemon juice to taste.

Nutty maple and vanilla granola
with homemade dried fruit

Philip and I met the year I was teaching French at the University of Illinois at Urbana-Champaign. Although we didn't date right away, food quickly brought us close: It started at the breakfast table. I remember thinking, "Wow, this guy has his priorities right!" Freshly sliced fruit, creamy plain yogurt and granola; some of my favorite morning foods were staple items on his table. It's funny, but in many ways, looking at what he was eating in the morning told me a lot about him. And right away, I liked him for that.

Over the years I've experimented with many granola recipes, like this maple and vanilla-flavored one in which I combine many different types of nuts. Use the kind of nuts you prefer and serve the granola with milk or yogurt, fresh and dried fruit, and honey or maple syrup.

*Makes 6 cups and many
happy breakfasts*

3 cups (300 g; 10 ½ oz) rolled oats

⅓ cup (50 g; 1 ¾ oz) pumpkin seeds

½ cup (50 g; 1 ¾ oz) pecans

⅓ cup (50 g; 1 ¾ oz) sunflower
    seeds

⅓ cup (50 g; 1 ¾ oz) slivered
    almonds

⅓ cup (50 g; 1 ¾ oz) sesame seeds

1 cup (100 g; 3 ½ oz) walnuts

½ cup (120 ml) water

½ cup (120 ml) maple syrup or
    honey

⅓ packed cup (55 g; 2 oz) light
    Muscovado sugar

1 tablespoon pure vanilla extract

½ teaspoon sea salt

¼ cup (60 ml) safflower or canola
    oil

Dried fruit like apple, cranberries,
    and cherries to taste (about
    1 cup)

Preheat the oven to 320°F (160°C). Cover a baking sheet with parchment paper; set aside.

In a large bowl, mix the rolled oats with the nuts and seeds; set aside. In a pot, heat the water, maple syrup, sugar, vanilla, sea salt, and oil over medium heat. Bring barely to a boil, then reduce the heat and simmer until the sugar is dissolved.

Add the wet ingredients to the dry ones and mix. Spread the mixture evenly on the baking sheet and bake for 50 minutes to 1 hour, until the granola is golden brown in color, stirring occasionally to make sure it bakes evenly. Remove from the oven and let cool to room temperature. Add the dried fruit. Serve with fresh fruit, yogurt, or milk, and honey or maple syrup if you like. This granola keeps well for 4 weeks stored in an airtight container.

It's easy to make your own dried fruit, like apples or strawberries. Pre-heat the oven to 220°F (100°C) and cover a baking sheet with parchment paper. Dust the paper with confectioners' sugar. Wash the fruit and pat it dry in a clean kitchen towel. Core the apples and hull the strawberries. Thinly slice the fruit (use a mandoline if you have one) and place the thin slices on the baking sheet. Dust again lightly with confectioners' sugar, place in the oven, and bake for 1 hour, rotating the baking sheet after 30 minutes. Take the baking sheet out of the oven and turn the slices over to the other side. Bake again for 30 to 40 minutes, checking regularly. The fruit should feel dry. Take one piece out and let it cool. If it's crunchy, it's ready. If not, continue to bake. When ready, let cool completely on a cooling rack. The fruit will keep for a few weeks stored in an airtight container.

Buttermilk, lemon, and poppy seed quinoa pancakes

"Let's do it!" Philip exclaimed when I pointed at photos of the house on my laptop. We were going to spend a week in Crete to celebrate our tenth wedding anniversary, and our baby, as I was also six months pregnant with Lulu. The house was simply gorgeous. It had a well-kept multilevel flower garden, olive trees, a long pool to rest by, and a fully equipped kitchen, which made me particularly happy. "No need to go anywhere!" I liked to joke when we sat down at the breakfast table to plan our day. I cooked our lunches and dinners with fresh produce from the local market in Chania—*hello, Greek salad and moussaka!*—and every morning, I made these pancakes. They are now one of Lulu's favorite breakfast foods. They are light and delicious, and always bring precious memories of that special time of our life.

I prefer to prepare my pancake batter with buttermilk, but have also used whole milk or plain yogurt before, depending on what I have handy. Serve the pancakes with warm maple syrup.

Makes ten to twelve 4-inch pancakes

⅓ cup (60 g; 2 oz) white rice flour or sweet rice flour
⅓ cup (40 g; 1 ½ oz) quinoa flour
⅓ cup (30 g; 1 oz) quinoa flakes
2 tablespoons blond cane sugar
1 teaspoon baking powder
½ teaspoon baking soda
2 pinches of sea salt
2 tablespoons poppy seeds
Finely grated zest of 1 organic lemon
2 large eggs, separated
1 cup (235 ml) buttermilk
½ teaspoon lemon extract (optional)
1 tablespoon canola oil, plus more to cook the pancakes

In a bowl, combine the flours, quinoa flakes, sugar, baking powder, baking soda, a pinch of sea salt, poppy seeds, and the lemon zest.

In another bowl, beat the egg yolks with the buttermilk. Beat in the lemon extract, if using, and the oil. Add this mixture to the dry ingredients and stir to combine.

In a third bowl, beat the egg whites with a pinch of sea salt until soft peaks form. Fold the whites into the batter.

In a frying pan, heat 1 tablespoon of canola oil over medium heat. Pour ¼ cup of batter in the pan and repeat for as many pancakes as the pan can hold. Cook until bubbles form on the surface, then flip the pancakes and continue to cook for 1 to 2 minutes, until golden.

Serve the pancakes with warm maple syrup or honey—Philip insists that the maple syrup has to be warm, so I'd better not leave this detail out—and fresh seasonal berries.

Cherry tomato tartlets tatin

Makes 4 tartlets

You will need: four 4 ½-inch tartlet molds

5 tablespoons olive oil, plus more
    for the molds and to serve
1 medium red onion, thinly sliced
1 bay leaf
2 thyme twigs
2 tablespoons dark Muscovado
    sugar
1 tablespoon balsamic vinegar
Sea salt and pepper
1 pound 5 oz (600 g) cherry toma-
    toes, cut in half and seeded
2 garlic cloves, minced
Brown rice, quinoa, and buckwheat
    crust (see Basic Recipes, page
    22, for instructions; note that
    you won't need the whole batch
    of crust for this recipe)
1 tablespoon chopped
    tarragon
10 thin slices of *manchego* cheese,
    or another rich sheep's milk
    cheese, plus more to serve
Baby arugula, to serve

These tomato tartlets are spectacular—addictively so! They follow the concept of a sweet *tarte tatin*—an apple tart baked upside down in which the apples develop a lovely caramel visible once you flip the tart onto a plate—but with the fruit and sugar replaced by cherry tomatoes, caramelized onions, and *manchego* cheese. These ingredients combined create such a delicious aroma while cooking that you won't be able to wait to eat the tartlets. If you like, you can prepare and assemble the ingredients one day ahead and bake the tart the next day.

Preheat the oven to 320°F (160°C). Oil four 4 ½-inch tartlet molds and set aside.

In a sauté pan, heat 2 tablespoons of the oil over medium heat. Add the onion, bay leaf, thyme, and 1 tablespoon of the sugar. Lower the heat to medium-low, cover, and cook for 15 minutes, stirring occasionally.

Add the vinegar, season with sea salt and pepper, and continue to cook, uncovered, for 15 more minutes. Remove from the heat, discard the bay leaf and thyme, and set aside.

In a bowl, gently toss the tomatoes with the garlic, the remaining 3 tablespoons oil, and the remaining 1 tablespoon sugar, and season with sea salt and pepper.

Place the tomatoes, cut side facing down, in a baking dish, place in the oven, and bake for about 30 minutes, until they look soft. Remove from the oven and set aside.

Roll your dough and cut 4 circles slightly bigger than the molds. Increase the heat of the oven to 350°F (180°C). Arrange the tomatoes in the molds, cut side facing up. Top with a layer of onion and sprinkle with the chopped tarragon. Finish with slices of cheese. Cover with a circle of dough, making sure to tuck the dough that goes over inside the mold, and make small holes on the surface of the dough with a fork.

Place the tartlets on a baking sheet before putting them in the oven. Place the tartlets in the oven and bake for about 30 minutes, until the crust is light brown in color. Remove the tartlets from the oven and let them cool for 5 minutes before unmolding them. To do so, put a plate on top of the mold and flip it over. Carefully remove the mold so that the tartlet is now open-faced. Repeat with the other three. To serve, top with arugula leaves and extra thin slices of cheese and drizzle with oil.

Millet, oat, and apple muffins

A plate filled with *still-warm-from-the-oven* muffins always lends a happy feel to our breakfast table. These muffins, in particular, are beautiful to start the day with—nutritious and healthy food that isn't too sweet. Invariably, the delicious aroma of baking throughout the house prompts us to rush to the table to eat.

Preheat the oven to 350°F (180°C). Line a muffin pan with 10 paper liners, or use silicone muffin molds; set aside.

In the bowl of a stand mixer, beat the eggs with the sugar; work until the texture is creamy and light in color and has doubled in size. Add the tahini, melted butter, and vanilla, and mix.

In a bowl, combine the millet and quinoa flours, the rolled oats, a pinch of sea salt, baking powder, and baking soda. Add to the batter, and using a wooden spoon, mix thoroughly, taking care not overwork the batter. Stir in the grated apple.

Divide the muffin batter among the muffin cases, topping each muffin with rolled oats. Bake the muffins for about 25 minutes, until golden and a knife inserted in the middle comes out clean.

Remove the muffins from the oven, invert them from the pan, and let cool on a wire rack.

Note: These can be kept for a few days in the fridge and then reheated in the oven or microwave; or they can be frozen.

Makes 10 muffins

2 large eggs

½ packed cup (80 g; 2 ¾ oz) light Muscovado sugar

2 tablespoons tahini (sesame butter)

3 ½ tablespoons (50 g; 1 ¾ oz) unsalted butter, melted

1 teaspoon pure vanilla extract

½ cup (60 g; 2 oz) millet flour

¼ cup (30 g; 1 oz) quinoa flour

½ cup (50 g; 1 ¾ oz) rolled oats, plus more for topping

Pinch of sea salt

1 teaspoon baking powder

½ teaspoon baking soda

1 cup (175 g, 6 oz) finely grated pink lady apples (from 2 apples, peeled and cored)

Oeufs en cocotte

with leeks, spinach, smoked salmon, and cumin

Serves 4

You will need: four 8-oz ramekins

2 tablespoons (30 g; 1 oz) unsalted butter

2 small young leeks, whites and greens, cleaned and thinly sliced diagonally

1 large shallot, finely chopped

¼ cup (60 ml) dry white wine or white vermouth

4 ½ oz (125 g, or 5 packed cups) fresh baby spinach

½ teaspoon ground cumin

Sea salt and pepper

2 large slices smoked salmon, minced

4 extra-fresh large eggs

6 tablespoons heavy cream

Freshly grated nutmeg

1 tablespoon chopped chives

Salmon roe, to serve (optional)

I have yet to tell you about my fascination with eggs. It's about the fond memory I have of collecting them at my grandmother's. It's about their beautiful natural shape, so simple and elegant, and so inspiring to style and photograph. And then there are the countless ways to cook them. One example is *oeufs en cocotte* (French for "baked eggs"). Eating this dish is a show in itself: You can dip a *mouillette* (the French word for "soldier," as in "a thin stick of bread") in the yellow of the runny egg yolk and watch the bread absorb it like a sponge, before popping the bread into your mouth. Then start all over again; it's exciting every time. These *oeufs en cocotte* offer delicate flavors of leek, smoked salmon, spices, cream, and butter that smell like a lazy brunch on a Sunday, though they are also perfect served as an appetizer. If you don't like a runny egg yolk, keep in mind that you can always adjust the cooking time to prepare the eggs the way you like.

Preheat the oven to 400°F (200°C). Butter four 8-oz ramekins; set aside.

In a frying pan, melt 1 tablespoon of the butter over medium heat. Add the leeks and shallot and cook on low to medium heat without browning, stirring, for about 7 minutes, until soft. Add the wine and cook until the liquid is absorbed; set aside.

Melt the remaining 1 tablespoon butter in the pan and add the spinach and cumin. Season with sea salt and pepper and cook for about 5 minutes, until the spinach is wilted. Let cool, and using your fingertips, squeeze the excess water. Finely chop and set aside.

In each ramekin, add a layer of leek, then one of smoked salmon. Finish with the spinach. Carefully break 1 egg inside each ramekin. Pour the cream around the egg yolk, making sure that it does not cover the yolk. Season with sea salt and pepper and add a pinch of nutmeg and chives. Cook the eggs in a water bath (see Basic Cooking Techniques, page 27, for instructions) for 10 to 12 minutes, until the egg white is set and the yolk is still runny. Serve warm with crusty bread or *mouillettes*, and if using, top with salmon roe.

Ratatouille tartlets
with poached eggs

Whenever I prepare *ratatouille*—I like to leave mine to stew for an hour and a half or longer—the rich scents that fill the kitchen have me dreaming about southern France. This *ratatouille* recipe is a shortcut for the days when I have less time to prepare the real thing. I fill savory crusts with the stewed vegetables and a few slices of cheese, add a poached egg on top, and serve the dish for brunch or a light lunch. It isn't quite the same as sitting at a café in a village in Provence, but I must say, it's pretty amazing too.

Note: The ratatouille, *like many stewed dishes, becomes even tastier the next day as the flavors develop.*

Preheat the oven to 350°F (180°C).

Roll and cut the dough to fit inside the tartlet molds. Arrange the dough inside each mold and using a fork, make small holes at the bottom. Prebake for 15 minutes (see Basic Cooking Techniques, page 27, for instructions). Remove the parchment paper and weights and continue to bake for 5 minutes. Remove from the oven and let cool.

Place the eggplant in a colander and sprinkle with sea salt. Leave for about 30 minutes, until some moisture releases. Pat the eggplant dry with paper towels.

In a large sauté pan, heat the oil over medium heat. Add the shallot and thyme and cook, without browning, for 2 minutes. Add the garlic and continue to cook for 1 minute, until fragrant. Add the eggplant, reduce the heat to medium-low, and cook for 5 minutes, stirring occasionally. Add the zucchini and peppers and continue to cook for 6 to 7 minutes, stirring occasionally, until just cooked through, then add the tomatoes, tomato paste, sugar, and bay leaf. Season with sea salt and pepper and add the tarragon. Simmer over medium-low heat, uncovered, for 25 minutes to 30 minutes, stirring occasionally, until the vegetables are soft and the juice is slightly reduced. Stir in the balsamic vinegar and cook for an extra minute. Remove from the heat and discard the thyme and bay leaf; set aside.

To poach the eggs, bring a large pot of water to a boil. Add the white wine vinegar and sea salt. Break each egg into a cup, and carefully transfer the eggs into the water. The water should barely be simmering. Cook for 2 to 3 minutes, until the white is set but the yolks are still runny. Carefully remove the eggs with a slotted spoon and place them on paper towels. Pat dry, and with a pair of scissors or knife, trim the egg whites to a shape you like.

To serve the dish, put a few slices of cheese into each crust and top with the warm vegetables and a poached egg, and finish with crushed red peppercorns. Serve with a side salad.

Makes six 4½-inch tartlets

You will need: six 4½-inch tartlet molds

Sweet rice, quinoa, and amaranth crust
 (See Basic Recipes, page 23)
1 medium Italian eggplant, diced into
 ¼-inch pieces
2 tablespoons olive oil
1 large shallot, finely chopped
2 thyme twigs
3 garlic cloves, minced
1 medium zucchini, diced into ¼-inch
 pieces
1 small red pepper, diced into ¼-inch
 pieces
1 small yellow pepper, diced into ¼-inch
 pieces
3 tomatoes, blanched, peeled, seeded,
 and cut into ½-inch pieces
1 tablespoon double-concentrated tomato
 paste
1 teaspoon dark Muscovado sugar
1 bay leaf
Sea salt and pepper
1 tablespoon chopped tarragon
1 tablespoon balsamic vinegar
2 oz (60 g) *manchego* cheese, thinly sliced
Crushed red peppercorns, to serve

For the poached eggs:
6 large eggs
1 tablespoon white wine vinegar
Pinch of sea salt

Chocolate crêpes

*Serves 4; makes ten to twelve
8-inch* crêpes

You will need: a *crêpe* pan

¾ cup (90 g; 3 oz) millet flour

4 tablespoons cornstarch

2 ½ tablespoons unsweetened cocoa
powder

2 tablespoons blond cane sugar

Pinch of sea salt

2 large eggs

1 ¼ cups (295 ml) whole milk

1 teaspoon pure vanilla extract

1 tablespoon (14 g; ½ oz) unsalted
butter, melted

Unsalted butter for the pan

To serve:

2 tablespoons (30 g; 1 oz) unsalted
butter

2 apples, peeled, cored, and thinly
sliced

3 to 4 tablespoons blond cane sugar,
to taste

Crème anglaise (see Basic Recipes,
page 26, using 1 teaspoon cornstarch)

Or:

Blond cane sugar, to sprinkle

Unsalted butter, softened

As a Frenchwoman, naturally I love *crêpes*. I find that *crêpes* are the tastiest street food you can enjoy when in France. *Crêpes* were also a weekly dinner my brother and I asked for when we were young—my mother never protested. She'd prepare hers with wheat flour, lightly sweetened, and make a stack that we'd enjoy with thinly sliced cooked apples, cocoa powder, or, my favorite, lemon juice and sprinkled sugar. Her *crêpes* were so thin, light, and delicious that no matter how tall the stack was, not a single crumb was ever left. For a twist on this classic, these *crêpes* are made with millet flour and flavored with chocolate. Serve them simply, sprinkled with sugar, or dress them up with a vanilla-flavored *crème anglaise* and thin slices of apples sautéed in butter. Or eat them as a snack during the day, whenever you walk by the kitchen, just as I—and Lulu—do.

Sift the flour, cornstarch, and cocoa powder into a large bowl. Mix in the sugar and sea salt and make a hole in the middle. Break the eggs into the hole and start to slowly pour in the milk while whisking. Continue until the batter is smooth. Stir in the vanilla and melted butter. (Alternatively, you can make the batter by blending all the ingredients in a food processor.) Cover the bowl with a plate and refrigerate for 2 hours. Bring back to room temperature before cooking and stir well again before using.

In a *crêpe* pan, melt ½ teaspoon of butter over medium heat. When the pan is hot, pour enough batter to cover the bottom (about ¼ cup). Swirl quickly to coat the bottom of the pan, and cook for 1 to 2 minutes, until small bubbles form at the surface. Using a spatula, flip the *crêpe* and cook on the other side for 1 minute. Transfer the *crêpe* to a plate and cover with a large piece of foil to keep warm. Add butter in the pan between each *crêpe*, and repeat until you run out of batter.

In a frying pan, melt the butter over medium-low heat.

Add the apple slices and sprinkle them with sugar. Raise the heat to medium and cook for 2 minutes, tossing with a spatula. Arrange the slices of apples on each *crêpe* before rolling them, or folding them into a triangle. Serve the *crêpes* with vanilla-flavored *crème anglaise*. Or simply eat them warm, sprinkled with blond cane sugar and a little piece of butter.

For a vanilla-flavored crêpe *variant, use exactly the same recipe without the cocoa powder. Sometimes, on the days when I cannot decide which ones I want to eat, I divide the batter and add chocolate to only half of it. This way you end up with both chocolate and vanilla* crêpes.

Basil-flavored zucchini and Comté muffins

This is so clever! I thought the first time I ate a savory muffin. I was living and teaching French in Wellington, New Zealand. Quickly nibbling on a savory muffin between my classes became a habit. Since then, I've extended my repertoire and experimented with many combinations of ingredients. Besides being a great choice for brunch, these muffins are delicious with a bowl of hearty soup for lunch.

Makes about 12 muffins

1 oz (30 g) hazelnuts, plus more for
   topping
3 large eggs
½ cup minus 1 tablespoon (100 ml)
   olive oil
½ cup minus 1 tablespoon (100 ml)
   buttermilk
1 cup (120 g; 4 ¼ oz) quinoa flour or
   millet flour
¾ cup (105 g; 3 ¾ oz) amaranth flour
1 teaspoon baking powder
½ teaspoon baking soda
Pinch of sea salt
3 oz (90 g) slices of uncured ham,
   chopped
2 oz (60 g) grated Comté cheese
2 medium zucchini (300 g;
   10 ½ oz), finely grated
1 tablespoon chopped basil
Pepper

For best grating results, use the smallest holes of a cheese grater to grate the zucchini.

Preheat the oven to 400°F (200°C). Line a muffin pan with 12 paper liners, or use silicone muffin molds if you prefer.

Toast the hazelnuts in a frying pan over medium heat for about 4 to 5 minutes, or until lightly browned and fragrant. Place them in a clean kitchen towel and rub them to remove the skins. When they are cool enough to be handled, chop them coarsely; set aside.

In a bowl, beat the eggs. Mix in the oil and buttermilk; set aside.

In a separate bowl, combine the flours with the baking powder, baking soda, and sea salt. Stir the flour mixture into the wet ingredients. Add the ham, cheese, zucchini, basil, and hazelnuts, season with pepper, and mix to incorporate all the ingredients.

Divide the batter among the muffin holes and top with a few hazelnuts. Place the muffins in the oven and bake for 10 minutes, then reduce the heat to 350°F (180°C) and bake for 15 to 20 more minutes, until a knife inserted in the middle comes out clean and they are golden. Remove the muffins from the oven and let them cool slightly in the pan before transferring them to a cooling rack. Cool completely before serving. They are lovely eaten at room temperature.

Comté is a French cheese made in the Franche–Comté region of eastern France. The cheese is made from unpasteurized cow's milk; it has a relatively hard texture, while the taste is slightly sweet and nutty. I always keep some in the fridge. If you cannot find it easily, I suggest replacing it with Gruyère or Emmenthal.

Sweet potato and carrot pancakes

I wasn't really sure what to call these the first time I made them. Somehow, they reminded me of a *blini* and the potato *râpés* (a French dish similar to a *latke*) my mother used to make at home. They also made me think of pancakes, except that here, they were savory. Lulu, in fact, inspired the recipe, as I was brainstorming ideas for her (only one year old then) to enjoy vegetables under a new form. She gobbled the pancake down so quickly that I was scared she was going to choke. The recipe has become a classic—enjoyed by children and adults alike—something we regularly have for brunch and lunch. Eat these plain or, for a more dressed-up version, serve them with a salad with a piquant hazelnut-flavored vinaigrette and toasted hazelnuts.

Makes six 3-inch pancakes

1 oz (30 g) hazelnuts
1 medium white sweet potato (or a regular sweet potato), peeled and diced
1 medium carrot, peeled and diced
Sea salt and pepper
2 large eggs, separated
3 tablespoons millet flour
3 tablespoons whole milk or buttermilk
1 tablespoon chopped cilantro
2 tablespoons olive oil, or as needed

Toast the hazelnuts in a frying pan over medium heat for about 4 to 5 minutes, or until lightly browned and fragrant. Place them in a clean kitchen towel and rub them to remove the skins. When they are cool enough to be handled, chop them coarsely; set aside.

Steam the sweet potato and carrot until soft. Using a food mill, purée the steamed vegetables. You should have 1 packed cup total puréed vegetables. Transfer to a large bowl and season with sea salt and pepper. Stir in the egg yolks, millet flour, milk, and cilantro. Mix until the ingredients are incorporated.

In the bowl of a stand mixer, beat the egg whites with a pinch of sea salt until they form soft peaks. Fold them into the vegetable mixture.

In a frying pan, heat the oil over medium heat. Drop ¼ cup of batter in the pan. Using the back of a spatula (rinse it under cold water to prevent it from sticking to the batter), flatten the pancake and cook for 2 to 3 minutes, then flip to the other side. Cook again for 2 to 3 minutes, until lightly browned on both sides. Repeat with the rest of the batter, adding more oil as needed. Top with the chopped hazelnuts and serve with a side salad, such as arugula or mâche.

Carrot, beet, and apple juice
with ginger and mint

"I've *never* actually had a glass of freshly squeezed apple juice!" my friend Rekha exclaimed dubiously when I handed her a glass full of juice. I had just freshly juiced a few organic green apples. She looked at the foam that had formed at the top and took a sip. I was watching, waiting for her reaction.

"Wow! That's actually really nice!"

This was just the way I felt. And I think you'll enjoy this juice too: The ginger and mint add an exotic touch, and it's full of vitamins.

Makes 2 cups, for 2 servings

You will need: a juicer

1 organic Granny Smith apple or
   other green apple
4 large organic carrots
1 medium (3 ½ oz; 100 g) organic
   beet, peeled and diced
½ inch piece fresh ginger, peeled and
   diced
Juice of ½ lime
5 or 6 mint leaves, or more, according to taste

Wash the fruit and vegetables. Juice the apple, carrots, beet, mint, and ginger in your juicer, according to the manufacturer's instructions. Add the lime juice and stir. Divide between 2 glasses and enjoy immediately.

Lunches to Inspire

I never skip lunch. *Ever.* It must be my upbringing that shaped me this way—you've probably heard the saying, that the French always take a long lunch, *blah blah blah.* Well, stereotype or not, it's true that lunch *is* special for the French. In my family, it's a warm meal that takes place between *midi* (noon) and 2 p.m., with all of us sitting around the table. If you happen to travel to smaller cities or villages in France, you'll quickly realize too—sometimes the hard way—that most places are closed at that time of the day; no one is expected to work at lunchtime.

When I still worked in an office, I'd make lunch a special occasion in the course of my day. It was a time to rejuvenate, relax, and think about something other than work. *Food,* what else was there? I remember sitting in the cafeteria and laying out my containers filled with leftovers from the night before, which consistently included an appetizer, main course, and dessert. It piqued my colleagues' curiosity. I remember them staring at the food with a *I-want-to-eat-that* look on their faces that made me smile each time. "*Ah ben alors,* you can do it too," I answered, feeling hungry. "Really, it's not that hard!" Tell me, why wouldn't someone want to take a well-deserved break during the day to shift from fast to slow gear? Everyone deserves it.

I probably like lunch as much as I like breakfast—and dinner, as a matter of fact. When friends are coming over, I dream up something simple: a dish of spiced spaghetti with fresh vegetables and tons of grated Parmesan; a quinoa *taboulé* (tabouli); or a vegetable tart—always with a green salad on the side. Most days, though, it's a bowl of homemade soup with a *tartine* that keeps me happy. I make sure to cook a large pot so that Philip, Lulu, and I can enjoy more over the course of a few days. Then, at other times, it's the thought of a picnic or a hike or a day at the beach that inspires me. I might prepare a potato salad, a thin omelet stuffed with crunchy vegetables, a carrot salad, or slices of a vegetable tart baked the day before. I'd pack this up with pieces of fruit, chocolate, a few muffins or cookies, and a thermos filled with warm tea to complete our meal—you cannot forget the tea!

"Have you always done this?" Philip asked once during the first year we were living together.

"What do you mean?" I replied, not sure I understood what he meant.

"Make lunch and bring it with you everywhere you go."

I looked at him and then laughed. *"Mais bien sûr!"* (Of course!) *"Après l'effort, il y a le réconfort!"* ("After the effort, comes the reward!") I added. "I cannot function if I don't eat a proper lunch, don't you know that yet?"

Of course he knew. And, after ten years of married life, he has come to see that very well.

Oh, the comfort of lunch!

A TARTINE AND
A BOWL OF SOUP

I met Tina by chance the first year I lived in Wellington. New
Zealand was always high on the list of places I dreamed of visiting, so the day I was offered a job to teach French at a high
school there, I didn't think twice about it. New Zealand was
calling my name! Tina and I quickly became best friends. "You
do the same silly things," her boyfriend, David, often told us
when we were all together. It was, and has stayed, an easy solid
friendship—besides sharing the same birthday, Tina and I
enjoy the same foods and the same things, like cooking! And
boy, is she a talented cook.

During the fall, she and I met every week to go horseback
riding. Since she had a car and I didn't, she'd stop by to pick
me up after work, and we'd drive forty-five minutes north of
Wellington into the countryside. I was always looking forward
to that moment in the week. I liked the chill in the air and the
exercise, the picturesque countryside with the smells of the
farm, but I was also looking forward to our lunch afterward.
On the way back, we invariably stopped at a small café, trying
a different one each time. We liked to share bowls of seasonal
soup with a vegetable muffin or a *tartine* on the side—I preferred

mine garnished with slices of roasted vegetables and fresh goat cheese. My favorite soup was the spicy butternut squash with apple cider and pieces of crumbled blue cheese sprinkled on top.

We swallowed our food slowly, each bite making our sore muscles relax.

"Mmmmmm, miam miam!" I'd tell Tina when our bowls of soup were licked clean. "I really want to make *that* at home."

She'd smile back. I knew she felt exactly the same way. A soup and a *tartine* were all we wanted.

Celeriac, white sweet potato, and apple soup
with parsley oil and marjoram

Serves 4

For the soup:

1 tablespoon (14 g; ½ oz) unsalted butter

1 tablespoon olive oil

1 small red onion, diced

2 garlic cloves, minced

12 oz (340 g) peeled and diced celeriac

8 ½ oz (240 g) peeled and diced white or regular sweet potato

1 large pink lady apple, peeled, cored, and diced

2 cups (475 ml) water

2 cups (475 ml) homemade vegetable broth (see Basic Recipes, page 25)

1 bay leaf

1 tablespoon marjoram leaves

Sea salt and pepper

⅔ cup (160 ml) heavy cream

Chopped flat-leaf parsley, to serve

Crumbles of blue cheese, to serve

For the parsley oil:

1 packed cup flat-leaf parsley leaves

⅔ cup (160 ml) olive oil

Sea salt

With its wrinkled, whitish skin and protruding stringy roots, celeriac (also known as celery root) won't win any beauty contests, but I nevertheless find it charming—perhaps because I'm French. In France, celeriac is commonly used in salads (like in the traditional *céleri rémoulade*, in which the vegetable is prepared raw, grated, and dressed in mayo), soups, gratins, or mashed. Hence, celeriac is the star of this soup recipe, though the blue cheese and parsley oil all play their part in creating the flavor.

To prepare the soup: In a heavy pot, melt the butter over medium heat. Add the oil and then the onion. Cook for 2 to 3 minutes, until soft. Add the garlic and continue to cook for 1 minute. Add the celeriac, sweet potato, and apple and cook, stirring, for 5 minutes. Add the water, stock, bay leaf, and marjoram and season with sea salt and pepper. Cover and simmer for 20 to 25 minutes, until the vegetables are fork-tender.

In the meantime, prepare the parsley oil: Blanch the parsley for 30 seconds in boiling salted water. Drain and squeeze out the excess water. Place the parsley in a blender with the oil and purée finely. Pass through a *chinois* or fine sieve and refrigerate until ready to use. This makes approximately ¼ cup of oil and will keep for 2 to 3 days in the fridge.

When the soup is ready, discard the bay leaf and transfer to the bowl of a food processor. Purée and return to the pot with the heavy cream. Reheat the soup and check the seasoning. Serve with crumbles of blue cheese, chopped parsley, and parsley oil.

When cleaning celeriac, remove the soft spongiest part that you can sometimes find in the middle when you slice the celeriac in half.

Jerusalem artichoke soup
with sautéed scallops and truffle oil

Serves 4

For the soup:

2 tablespoons olive oil

2 shallots or 1 small red onion, finely chopped

¼ teaspoon coriander seeds, finely crushed

1 thyme twig

2 celery stalks, diced

1 pound 7 oz (650 g) Jerusalem artichokes (sunchokes), peeled and diced

1 medium Yukon gold potato, peeled and diced

1 bay leaf

Sea salt and pepper

4 cups (945 ml) water or homemade vegetable broth (see Basic Recipes, page 25)

4 tablespoons *crème fraîche*, *mascarpone* cheese, or heavy cream

1 tablespoon chopped flat-leaf parsley, plus more to serve

For the scallops:

1 tablespoon olive oil

24 small bay scallops

Truffle oil, to serve

Fleur de sel, to serve

In the winter of 2008 Philip and I took to a fantastic trip to Copenhagen. I remember walking through the Danish capital's windy streets for hours, excited and happy, even when we felt cold and hungry. We'd stop in at cafés, warming up with a cup of steaming tea or a bowl of soup. One day, it was a Jerusalem artichoke soup served with scallops that we ordered. It was particularly freezing out that day, but the taste of the soup made us forget our frozen feet. It was so delicious that before we were even done with the first bowl we each ordered a second one, keen to keep the taste with us. That moment inspired me to make this soup once we returned home. I'll never forget how it ended up on our table.

To prepare the soup: In a large heavy pot, heat the oil over medium heat. Add the shallots, coriander seeds, and thyme and sauté, without browning, for 2 to 3 minutes, until soft and fragrant. Add the rest of the vegetables and the bay leaf, season with salt and pepper, and cook for about 6 minutes, until the vegetables have softened, stirring occasionally. Add the water or broth and bring to a boil. Cover and simmer for 20 to 25 minutes, until the vegetables are fork-tender. Remove from the heat and discard the thyme and bay leaf. Transfer the soup to the bowl of a food processor and purée finely. Stir in the *crème fraîche* and parsley.

To prepare the scallops: Heat the oil in a frying pan over medium heat. Quickly cook the scallop—only 30 seconds for small ones—until just lightly cooked. The longer they cook, the less tender they become.

To serve, divide the soup among bowls and top with the scallops and parsley. Add a drizzle of truffle oil and a pinch of *fleur de sel*.

A Jerusalem artichoke is neither an artichoke, nor is it grown in Jerusalem—the name is somewhat of a mystery. It's also known as a sunchoke. It's a crisp vegetable with a flavor that's somewhere between an artichoke heart and a sunflower seed. It's excellent fried, in a salad, mashed—and in soups.

Fennel and green pea soup
with wasabi-flavored whipped cream and sautéed shrimp

Though I've made this soup at lunch just for myself, it's so pretty that it really deserves to be shared with company. And though it may sound fancy, it's quite simple to prepare. The delicate pea broth paired with earthy-flavored shrimp and spiced up with wasabi cream make the soup a beautiful way to begin a dressed-up meal. And the Sichuan pepper gives it a unique aroma with slight lemony overtones. It's a refreshing and colorful soup, and you'll love it for that too!

Serves 4

You will need: four 4-inch ring molds

For the fennel and pea soup:
1 tablespoon (14 g; ½ oz) unsalted butter
1 tablespoon olive oil
1 shallot, finely chopped
½ teaspoon fennel seeds, finely crushed
1 leek, white part only, finely chopped
3 garlic cloves, minced

1 large fennel bulb (250 g; 8 ¾ oz), greens and core discarded, sliced
4 cups (945 ml) good-quality organic chicken stock
Sea salt and pepper
Dash of Sichuan pepper (ground in a pepper mill)
3 cups (390 g; 14 oz) fresh or frozen peas

For the wasabi cream garnish:
¼ cup (60 ml) cold heavy cream
¼ teaspoon wasabi paste
Dash of sea salt
1 tablespoon chopped chervil

For the shrimp garnish:
1 tablespoon safflower oil
1 garlic clove, minced
Dash of ground cumin
12 large shrimp, peeled and deveined
Sea salt and pepper

To prepare the soup: In a heavy pot, melt the butter over medium heat. Add the olive oil, then add the shallot, fennel seeds, and leek and cook for 3 to 4 minutes, stirring, without browning, until the aromas start to come out. Add the garlic and cook for 1 more minute. Add the fennel and cook, stirring occasionally, for 5 minutes, until the fennel softens. Pour in the chicken stock, season with sea salt and the Sichuan pepper, and simmer until the vegetables are fork-tender, 20 to 25 minutes. Add the peas and cook for 5 more minutes, until they are bright green but no longer raw.

Remove from the heat and transfer the soup to the bowl of a food processor. Purée the soup and pass it through a fine sieve,

pressing on the pea skins to remove as much purée as possible. The broth will be thin. Adjust the seasoning with sea salt and pepper.

Meanwhile, prepare the wasabi cream: Beat the cream with the wasabi and sea salt. When the cream forms soft peaks, add the chervil and continue to beat for 10 more seconds.

To prepare the shrimp: Heat the safflower oil in a frying pan over high heat. Add the garlic, cumin, and shrimp, and cook quickly, stirring, for 1 minute on each side. Season with sea salt and pepper. Remove from the heat and let cool. When they are cool enough handle, dice 8 of the shrimp, discarding the tails, and keep the other 4 shrimp whole; set aside.

To serve, reheat the pea soup over medium heat. Take 4 shallow bowls and place a 4-inch ring mold in the middle. Divide the chopped shrimp into the 4 molds and top each with one of the whole shrimp. Ladle the pea broth around the shrimp, remove the molds, and serve the soup with a dollop of wasabi-flavored cream.

Carrot and red lentil soup

with coconut milk

I have a weakness for the sweetness of a carrot soup. So much so that many pages of my cooking notebook are filled with carrot recipes of all kinds. Some are mild and uncomplicated, the way my mother used to make hers, while others suggest an unusual pairing of ingredients, like this one made with red lentils and coconut milk, which I am particularly fond of. It's a nutritious soup that gets even better with time.

In a large heavy pot, melt the butter over medium heat. Add the oil, then add the onion, leek, cumin, and thyme and cook for 3 to 4 minutes, stirring, until fragrant and the onion is soft. Add the garlic and cook for 1 more minute. Add the tomato and tomato paste and cook for 2 to 3 more minutes, until the tomato has softened. Add the carrots, lentils, cold water, and bay leaf and season with sea salt and pepper. Cover and simmer for about 20 minutes, until the vegetables and lentils are soft.

Remove from the heat, discard the bay leaf, and transfer the soup to the bowl of a food processor; purée until smooth. Return the soup to the pot and stir in the coconut milk. Reheat and check the seasoning for coconut milk and sea salt and pepper. Serve in bowls with a squeeze of lime juice, cilantro, and crushed red peppercorns.

Serves 4

1 tablespoon (14 g; ½ oz) unsalted butter

2 tablespoons olive oil

1 red onion, sliced

1 leek, white part only, finely chopped

1 teaspoon ground cumin

1 teaspoon finely chopped thyme

2 garlic cloves, minced

1 large vine tomato, blanched, peeled, seeded, and diced

1 tablespoon double-concentrated tomato paste

2 cups (300 g; 10 ½ oz) peeled and sliced carrots (from 4 to 5 carrots)

1 cup (175 g: 6 ¼ oz) dried red lentils, rinsed and sorted

4 cups (945 ml) cold water

1 bay leaf

Sea salt and pepper

¾ cup (175 ml) unsweetened coconut milk, or more to taste

Lime juice, to serve

Chopped cilantro, to serve

Crushed red peppercorns, to serve

Cold honeydew and cucumber soup

with its colorful skewers

Serves 6

You will need: 6 small skewers

1 pound 7 oz (650 g) honeydew
　　melon flesh, diced
1 long English cucumber (300 g;
　　10 ½ oz), peeled, cut in half,
　　seeded, and diced
1 shallot, peeled and finely chopped
Juice of 1 large orange or ¼ cup apple
　　juice
Juice of 1 lime
15 purple or African blue basil leaves
Sea salt and pepper
2 tablespoons olive oil, plus more for
　　drizzling

For the skewers:
3 balls of fresh mozzarella or 6 mini
　　mozzarella balls
¼ honeydew melon
¼ watermelon, seeded
¼ cantaloupe melon
Purple basil leaves
3 slices of prosciutto, cut in half
　　lengthwise
Pepper

I don't often go out for lunch alone, but when I do, something special always happens. Like the day when I ate a cold melon soup in the restaurant Pères et Filles in the 6th arrondissement of Paris. The taste of the soup was so sweet and delicate that despite trying to eat slowly to prolong the moment, I gobbled my bowl down in less than a minute, keen to return to my kitchen to make my own version.

This cold soup is wonderful on a hot summer day. You can dress it up by adding skewers of mozzarella, prosciutto, and different types of colorful melon, which is sure to impress your friends. Note that to get the best results, it's preferable to choose the most fragrant and ripe fruit that you can find.

In the bowl of a food processor, combine the honeydew, cucumber, shallot, orange and lime juice, and basil leaves and pulse into a fine purée. Season with sea salt and pepper and stir in the oil. Transfer to a bowl, cover, and refrigerate for a few hours, until chilled.

To prepare the skewers: Use a melon scoop to shape small balls of mozzarella, honeydew, watermelon, and cantaloupe. On each skewer, alternate the following ingredients, adding a basil leaf between each: 2 balls of cantaloupe, 1 ball of watermelon, 1 ball of honeydew, and 2 balls of mozzarella wrapped in half a slice of prosciutto. Season with pepper.

To serve, ladle the soup into shallow bowls or small glasses and drizzle with oil. Serve with the skewers.

Tartine

with fava beans, poppy seed goat cheese, and lemon vinaigrette

With their delicate buttery taste, fava beans are among the foods that make me crave the first days of spring. These beautiful bright green beans are excellent sautéed in a little olive oil, used in risottos, or for dressing up a *tartine*. Perhaps you'll find that using the beans fresh is labor-intensive in preparation, but after you taste one, you won't think twice about it. It's worth all the effort you put into it.

Makes 4 tartines

2 cups shelled fava beans
    (from 2 pounds in the pod)
Sea salt
4 oz (120 g) soft fresh goat cheese
1 tablespoon whole milk
1 tablespoon poppy seeds
4 slices of *pain de campagne*
    (country bread)
¼ orange bell pepper, seeds and
    white membranes removed,
    thinly sliced

For the dressing:
Sea salt and pepper
1 tablespoon lemon juice
½ teaspoon honey
1 garlic clove, minced
1 tablespoon olive oil
1 tablespoon pecan, hazelnut, or
    walnut oil

For the garnish:
Thin slices of shaved pecorino
A few fresh mint leaves

Bring a large pot of water to boil. Add a generous pinch of sea salt and blanch the fava beans for 1 minute. Drain, rinse them under cold water, and let cool. When they are cool enough to handle, carefully remove the skin around the beans; transfer to a bowl.

In another bowl, combine the goat cheese, milk, and poppy seeds and work into a smooth paste, adding more milk if necessary to reach a texture you can spread easily. Toast the pieces of bread and spread the cheese on top.

In a small bowl, combine the sea salt and pepper, then add the lemon juice and honey. Stir in the garlic, then whisk with the olive and pecan oils. Pour the dressing over the fava beans and toss gently.

To serve, arrange the beans and pepper slices on top of the *tartines,* and top with slices of pecorino and mint leaves, adding more dressing if needed.

Tartine

with walnut, lemon, and ricotta pesto and sautéed mushrooms

> I remember making this *tartine* one winter day when it was particularly cold outside and I had a craving for melting cheese. In my fridge, I had leftover ricotta from a dish of lasagna we had eaten the night before—and a box of mushrooms. Without any outlined plan, I decided to improvise this original pesto, letting my imagination and taste buds lead the way to what was going to become lunch. And that's how I ended up with this delectable *tartine,* which I enjoyed with a bowl of warm celeriac soup. It was pure bliss.

Makes 4 tartines

For the walnut, lemon, and ricotta pesto:
1 garlic clove, peeled and crushed
2 tablespoons (30 g; 1 oz) walnuts
½ packed cup flat-leaf parsley
Finely grated zest of ½ organic lemon
Pinch of sea salt
2 tablespoons olive oil
4 tablespoons fresh whole milk ricotta cheese

For the mushrooms:
1 tablespoon olive oil
1 cup thinly sliced cremini mushrooms
Sea salt and pepper

4 slices of country bread
Dash of freshly grated nutmeg
1 oz (30 g) finely grated cheddar cheese

To make the walnut pesto: In the bowl of a food processor, combine the garlic, walnuts, parsley, lemon zest, and sea salt and pulse to finely chop. Add the oil and continue to work to obtain a paste. Transfer the paste to a bowl and combine with the ricotta; set aside.

To make the mushrooms: In a frying pan, heat the oil over medium heat. Add the mushrooms, season with sea salt, and sauté until the mushrooms release their juice. Remove from the heat and season with pepper.

Preheat the broiler. Toast the bread and spread with the pesto-flavored ricotta. Top with the mushrooms, nutmeg, and grated cheese. Place the *tartines* under the broiler until the cheese melts—this takes 2 to 3 minutes, depending how close the flame is to the *tartines*. Serve immediately with your favorite soup, if you like.

Tartine

with tarragon–flavored slow-roasted cherry tomatoes and prosciutto

Slow-roasted tomatoes come in handy for many dishes: to flavor a dish of pasta, to accompany a piece of grilled meat, or, like here, on a *tartine*. I make sure to choose perfectly ripe cherry tomatoes, and I like to flavor them with tarragon—this gives them a rich sweet licorice aroma that is balanced by the slightly salty taste of prosciutto. When I feel like a burst of summery flavors in my mouth, this is the *tartine* I choose.

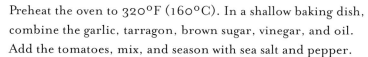

Preheat the oven to 320°F (160°C). In a shallow baking dish, combine the garlic, tarragon, brown sugar, vinegar, and oil. Add the tomatoes, mix, and season with sea salt and pepper.

Place in the oven and bake for 1 to 1 ½ hours, until the tomatoes are soft. Toast the bread and spread with the goat cheese. Top each *tartine* with 2 slices of prosciutto and a few tomatoes. Drizzle with oil and sprinkle with *fleur de sel*.

Makes 4 tartines

2 garlic cloves, minced

1 teaspoon finely chopped
    tarragon

1 teaspoon light Muscovado sugar

1 tablespoon balsamic vinegar

¼ cup (60 ml) olive oil, plus more to
    drizzle

9 oz (250 g) ripe cherry
    tomatoes

Sea salt and pepper

4 slices of your favorite country
    bread

½ cup (100 g; 3 ½ oz) soft fresh goat
    cheese, to spread

8 slices of prosciutto

Fleur de sel, to serve

Tartine

with citrus avocado and cumin-flavored shrimp

In New England, the season for Maine shrimp is short, so when I find this tasty variety of shrimp at my market, I make sure to find original ways to cook them—like this recipe where they look particularly cute arranged on top of a *tartine*—they are perfect in size for this kind of food. The sweet delicate flavor of the shrimp pairs perfectly with the warm taste of cumin and the buttery texture of the avocado.

Makes 4 tartines

1 ripe avocado

½ tablespoon lime juice

2 tablespoons olive oil

1 teaspoon chopped cilantro

Pinch of sea salt

Dash of cayenne pepper

¼ teaspoon ground cumin

1 garlic clove, finely chopped

24 small shrimp (preferably from Maine), peeled and deveined

4 slices of rye or whole wheat bread

4 leaves Bibb lettuce

In a bowl, mash the avocado with a fork. Add the lime juice, 1 tablespoon of the oil, and the cilantro, and season with sea salt and the cayenne; mix well. Taste and adjust the seasoning to your liking.

In a frying pan, heat the remaining 1 tablespoon oil over medium heat. Add the cumin and garlic and cook for 1 minute, without browning. Raise the heat to medium-high, add the shrimp, and cook for only 1 to 2 minutes, stirring. Remove from the heat and set aside.

Spread the avocado mixture over the slices of bread (I prefer this type of bread not toasted, but you can choose what you like best). Top each *tartine* with a lettuce leaf and a few shrimp.

LE PIQUE-NIQUE (THE PICNIC)

In many ways, I am like my father. We are both tall with dark green eyes; we are the only ones in the family who like to snack on hard-boiled eggs; we cannot memorize historical dates (unlike my mother and brother); we thrive on cold snowy winters; we are countryside people at heart and like to pick mushrooms in the fields wearing our Wellington boots. We are also the planners in the family. I didn't always acknowledge this, but somehow, I think it's my father who passed that skill on to me. It comes in handy when planning the foods to bring along on a trip or an excursion.

When we first met, Philip didn't always see the point in this kind of planning. He looked puzzled as he'd watch me pack large bags of groceries for an outing, and I'd never fail to ask, "What kind of sandwich do you want?" He'd argue that he couldn't think about it *then* or that we didn't need all that extra gear. "We'll figure it out" was his answer. But over time he realized that planning what we were going to eat was useful when we were in the middle of nowhere with rumbling bellies.

To have a backpack filled with treats when we go hiking, for example, is a highlight of our excursion. It might contain a quinoa salad; slices of potato tortilla; a carrot salad dressed with lemon, olive oil, and mint; a few bags of chips; sandwiches filled with avocado, marinated cucumber, and smoked salmon; and a slice of homemade cake. When fellow hikers walk by and comment on our food with an envious look on their faces, we smile.

"I *told* you!" I'd say to Philip with a victorious look on my face.

Needless to add that I am now free to pack what I see fit without my beloved husband saying a word about it. Instead he gives me approving smiles.

He likes it as much as I do.

Omelet wraps

with nori and crunchy vegetables

I used the idea behind a *crêpe* to invent these tasty omelet wraps. They are stuffed with crunchy vegetables, thinly sliced to reveal more flavor, and use the omelet as the wrap. You can also slice the omelet into smaller pieces and serve them on toothpicks as hors d'oeuvre at a party.

Makes 2 thin omelets; serves 4

For the omelets:
6 large eggs
2 tablespoons chopped flat-leaf
    parsley
2 tablespoons chopped chives
2 nori sheets, thinly sliced (use a pair
    of scissors)
Sea salt and pepper
About 3 tablespoons olive oil

For the vinaigrette:
Sea salt and pepper
1 teaspoon French Dijon mustard
1 tablespoon Banyuls vinegar
2 tablespoons hazelnut oil
1 tablespoon olive oil

For the filling:
2 heaping tablespoons (1 ½ oz;
    40 g) walnuts
6 oz (180 g) red cabbage, thinly
    sliced (makes 2 cups once sliced)

2 carrots, peeled and julienned
1 Belgian endive, heart removed and
    thinly sliced lengthwise
1 avocado, peeled, pitted, and thinly
    sliced, drizzled with lemon juice
    to prevent discoloration
1 tablespoon finely chopped chives,
    plus a few more long pieces to tie
    the omelets
2 oz (60 g) crumbled French feta
    cheese

Nori is a type of edible seaweed that is shredded and dried into sheets. It is common in Japanese cuisine, especially for wrapping sushi. It can be found in the Asian section of your supermarket.

To prepare the omelets: In a bowl, beat the eggs. Add the herbs and nori and season with salt and pepper. In a 14-inch non-stick frying pan, heat 1 to 2 tablespoons oil over medium heat. Add half of the egg batter, swirling quickly to coat the bottom of the pan, and cook for a few minutes, until the omelet is set. Carefully transfer the omelet onto a plate or cutting board. Repeat with the rest of the egg batter to prepare the second omelet, adding more oil as needed.

To prepare the vinaigrette: Add the ingredients to a bowl in the order listed. Whisk to emulsify the dressing; set aside.

To prepare the filling: Toast the walnuts in a frying pan over medium heat for about 5 minutes, or until fragrant and lightly brown. Remove from the heat, let cool, and coarsely chop; set aside.

In a bowl, combine the cabbage, carrots, endive, avocado, and chives. Dress with the vinaigrette and add the walnuts and feta. Place one omelet flat in front of you and add half of the filling at one end. Roll the omelet tight and cut in half. Tie each half with a long piece of chive. Repeat with the second omelet.

Potato, Jerusalem artichoke, spinach, and asparagus frittata with cumin

I fell in love with *tortilla de patatas españolas* (the famous Spanish thick omelet of eggs and potatoes and onion cooked in olive oil) the year Philip and I attended our friends Susanna and Fernando's wedding in Segovia. Every morning, that's what we ate for breakfast. I prefer to cook a tortilla the way I do a frittata, its close cousin, as I find that finishing it in the oven makes for a prettier dish—besides, it's much easier. However, both are equally delicious. This frittata is prepared with Jerusalem artichokes, also known as sunchokes, whose sweet artichokelike flavor gives it new life and character. When we travel or have a picnic, this is what I like to bring along. It's also a dish that you'll enjoy for brunch or, if sliced into smaller squares, as finger food for a party. It's also the type of food that is easily customized, welcoming many other vegetables, and even meat, so feel free to substitute and try different things.

Makes one 9-inch frittata; serves 8

Ten 2-inch-long green asparagus tips

Sea salt

⅓ cup (80 ml) olive oil

1 packed cup (50 g; 1¾ oz) spinach leaves

1 red onion, thinly sliced

7 oz (200 g) russet potatoes (about 2 medium potatoes), peeled and sliced

7 oz (200 g) Jerusalem artichokes (about 5), peeled and sliced

8 large eggs

1 teaspoon ground cumin

Pepper

1 tablespoon chopped cilantro

Blanch the asparagus tips in boiling salted water for 2 minutes so they turn bright green, then drain and rinse under cold water; set aside.

In an 8-inch nonstick frying pan, heat 1 tablespoon of the oil. Add the spinach and cook for 2 minutes, or until wilted. Remove from the heat, let cool, and finely chop; set aside.

In the same skillet, heat ¼ cup of the remaining oil over medium heat. Add the onion, reduce the heat to medium-low, and cook for 4 to 5 minutes, without browning, stirring, until soft. Add the potatoes and Jerusalem artichokes and cook, without browning, for about 20 minutes, stirring, until the vegetables are tender. Transfer to a bowl.

In another bowl, beat the eggs and cumin with a fork and season with sea salt and pepper. Stir in the potatoes, Jerusalem artichokes, spinach, asparagus, and cilantro.

Preheat the broiler.

Heat the remaining 1 tablespoon oil in the same skillet over medium heat. Add the egg and vegetable batter. Cook the frittata for about 7 to 8 minutes, until the edges and bottom of the egg batter start to set—the middle will still be fairly runny.

Place the frittata under the broiler and broil until the egg batter is finished setting, about 4 minutes. Remove from the oven and transfer to a plate. Let cool slightly and slice the tortilla into wedges. It's best to eat the frittata at room temperature.

French carrot salad
with fresh herbs

A simple grated carrot salad is not only *very* French, but it's a dish that my father and I could literally eat with every meal—which invariably drives my mother crazy. This salad is honest food at its best, handy to make for any occasion. So simple. So zesty and colorful. I find that the flavor of the salad is improved when the carrots are finely grated—julienned; and once again, using fresh organic carrots makes for the most flavorful salad.

Using the finest slicing attachment of your food processor, grate the carrots; or use a regular manual grater if you prefer. Transfer the carrots to a bowl.

To prepare the vinaigrette: In a separate bowl, combine the ingredients in the order listed. Whisk to emulsify. Dress the carrots with the vinaigrette. Cover and refrigerate.

When ready to serve, add the fresh herbs and mix well.

Serves 4

4 large carrots (500 g; 1 pound plus
   2 oz), peeled
1 tablespoon chopped flat-leaf
   parsley
2 tablespoons chopped chives

For the vinaigrette:
Sea salt and pepper
¼ cup (60 ml) fresh lemon juice
1 garlic clove, minced
6 tablespoons olive oil

Fingerling potato salad
with peas, radishes, and quail eggs

I am lucky. My mother is not only a great cook, someone who feeds her love through her food, but she also makes the best *salades de pommes de terre* (potato salad). She prepares hers with *ratte* potatoes (a French variety similar to fingerlings) she grows in her garden, nice in a salad because their pretty shape stays intact. This recipe is one of the many *salades de pommes de terre* that I enjoy preparing. You can add French mustard to the vinaigrette for a dressing that is more piquant. I sometimes also add fresh marinated anchovies and black olives.

Serves 4

2 tablespoons pine nuts

1 small red onion, thinly sliced

Sea salt

12 quail eggs (use 4 chicken eggs if you cannot find quail eggs)

1 cup (130 g; 4 ½ oz) shelled green peas (fresh or frozen)

1 ½ pounds (675 g) organic fingerling potatoes

4 French pink breakfast radishes or regular pink radishes, thinly sliced

1 tablespoon chopped chives

2 tablespoons chopped flat-leaf parsley

2 tablespoons chopped basil

Pepper

For the vinaigrette:

Sea salt and pepper

1 teaspoon French Dijon mustard

3 tablespoons lemon juice

⅓ cup (80 ml) olive oil

Toast the pine nuts in a frying pan over medium heat for 2 minutes, or until lightly colored and fragrant. Set aside to cool.

Soak the onion in a bowl of cold salted water for 20 minutes. Drain and pat dry.

Boil the quail eggs for 3 minutes. Drain and rinse under cold water to stop them from cooking. Shell the eggs and cut each in half (quail eggs are slightly more delicate than chicken eggs, so go slow). If you use chicken eggs, increase the cooking time to 6 minutes. Once shelled, quarter them.

Boil the green peas in salted water for 3 minutes. Drain and rinse them under cold water to stop them from cooking and let them cool.

Steam the potatoes for about 15 minutes, until they are cooked through. Drain and let them cool slightly, then peel and cut them into ½-inch slices.

To prepare the vinaigrette: In a small bowl, combine the ingredients in the order listed. Whisk together to emulsify.

In a large bowl, combine the potatoes, onions, peas, eggs, and radishes. Dress with the vinaigrette, herbs, and pine nuts, and season with sea salt and pepper. Toss well and serve.

Note: If you make the salad ahead of time, you might need to add a little more oil before serving.

Vitamin-boosted black rice salad

"How pretty and dramatic!" I remember thinking the first time I cooked with black rice. This kind of rice has a nutty flavor and purplish black color that beautifies any rice salad. Although somewhat harder to find, it's a favorite grain in my pantry—its taste is rich and earthy in the mouth, and it's extremely nutritious, giving you a boost of iron with every mouthful.

To prepare the vinaigrette: In a small bowl, combine the ingredients in the order listed. Whisk to emulsify.

To prepare the salad: Toast the walnuts in a frying pan over medium heat for 5 minutes, or until fragrant and lightly browned. Remove from the heat and let cool. Chop coarsely and set aside. Cook the rice according to the instructions on the package. Check whether it's well cooked and drain if there's still water in the pot; let cool. With a sharp serrated knife, peel the skin and pith from the grapefruit. Cut the fruit into segments, discarding the membrane; dice, cover, and set aside until ready to serve.

In a large bowl, combine the rice, fennel, grapes, grapefruit, cheese, and walnuts. Toss the salad gently with the dressing and fresh herbs and serve.

Serves 4

For the vinaigrette:

Sea salt and pepper

1 teaspoon French Dijon
     mustard

1 teaspoon honey

2 tablespoons sherry vinegar

6 tablespoons olive oil

For the salad:

1 oz (30 g) walnuts

1 cup (200 g; 7 oz) black rice

1 pink grapefruit or 1 orange

1 fennel bulb, without greens, cored
     and sliced paper-thin (use a man-
     doline if you have one)

1 cup (100 g; 3 ½ oz) red grapes, cut
     in half

2.5 oz (70 g) feta cheese,
     crumbled

1 tablespoon chopped flat-leaf
     parsley

1 tablespoon chopped chives

1 tablespoon chopped dill

Beet and quinoa tabouli

Tabouli is commonly prepared with couscous, but I prefer the salad when quinoa is used instead. The natural dye of beets adds a cheerful pink hue to this tabouli that makes the salad stand out on your plate. Add colorful cherry tomatoes picked right off the vine or bought at your local farmers' market, a handful of fresh herbs with lemon juice and olive oil, and you're guaranteed to have what I like to think of as the perfect summer lunch.

Note: If you want to give the quinoa extra flavor, use vegetable broth rather than water.

Serves 4 to 6

2 tablespoons pine nuts

1 cup (200 g; 7 oz) uncooked white quinoa

2 cups (475 ml) water or homemade vegetable broth (see Basic Recipes, page 25)

Sea salt

1 large cooked beet, peeled and diced

1 cup mixed cherry tomatoes, cut in half

¼ red onion, finely chopped

3 oz (90 g) feta cheese, crumbled

For the vinaigrette:

Sea salt and pepper

Juice of 1 lemon or lime

6 tablespoons olive oil

2 tablespoons chopped flat-leaf parsley

1 tablespoon chopped cilantro

1 tablespoon chopped chives

1 tablespoon chopped mint

Toast the pine nuts in a frying pan over medium heat for 2 minutes, or until lightly colored and fragrant; remove from the heat and set aside to cool.

Rinse the quinoa under cold water and drain it in a colander. Add it to a pot and cover with the water or broth and a pinch of sea salt. Bring to a boil, then turn down the heat, cover, and simmer for 12 to 14 minutes, or until all of the water or broth is absorbed. Remove from the heat and keep covered for 5 more minutes. Transfer the quinoa to a bowl and fluff it with a fork; let cool. Add the beet and toss gently. The quinoa will take on a nice pink color. Add the tomatoes, onion, and cheese.

To prepare the vinaigrette: In a small bowl, combine the sea salt and pepper with the lemon juice and oil, and whisk to emulsify. Stir in the herbs. Dress the salad with this vinaigrette and adjust the seasoning to your taste. Add more dressing if you like and serve with the pine nuts.

To cook the beet (unpeeled), you have two options: Add it to a pot of water, bring to a boil, and cook until it's easy to insert a knife in the middle. Or you can wrap it in aluminum foil and bake it in an oven preheated to 375°F (190°C). The cooking time depends on the size of the beet — it can take between 40 minutes and 1 hour — check regularly. Once cooked through, let cool before peeling the beet.

Zucchini salad
with fresh herbs

"I want the recipe!" my friend Kristen said the first time she ate this salad at my house. It had never occurred to me before that I could actually write down the recipe: It was so simple! But so delicious too! Slicing the zucchini spaghetti-style is what makes this salad special. Feel free to add more ingredients to bring even more flavors to the salad: feta cheese, for example, would be excellent in it.

To make the dressing: In a small bowl, add the ingredients in the order listed. Whisk to emulsify.

Dress the zucchini with the vinaigrette and toss the fresh herbs in. Mix well and refrigerate until ready to serve.

Serves 4

For the vinaigrette:
Sea salt and pepper
2 tablespoons white wine vinegar
1 garlic clove, minced
1 teaspoon maple syrup or honey
6 tablespoons good-quality olive oil

2 zucchini, finely julienned (use a mandoline if you have one)
¼ cup chopped fresh herbs (such as mint, parsley, and chervil)

CASUAL LUNCHES
WITH FRIENDS

I invariably feel touched when a friend calls to ask if I want to come over for lunch. It's a simple thing really, but every time it happens, I feel the same eagerness. I am happy. And hungry to taste someone else's cooking.

Lunch conveys a different feel, somehow more charming than dinner. Don't you think so too? Perhaps it's because by inviting me, that friend is telling me, "I am stopping what I am doing today and I have decided to cook and spend the day with you." Because lunch is surely going to put a stop to what was planned during the day. And the focus of the day will be around the time we spend together, our conversations to catch up and discuss events in our lives—and homemade foods. What else?

So naturally, I am a lover of lunches we spend with friends. Casual and down to earth, with colorful foods that we will share with the people who are special in our life. When I am the one inviting, it's most likely a vegetable tart, a hearty soup, a dish of spaghetti or quinoa, a risotto, or a tomato *clafoutis* that I'll be making. And for dessert, there will be a fruit salad, a chocolate mousse, a verrine, a fruit tart, or a cake to finish our meal—something tasty and pretty, and quick to prepare too. When lunch is over, we will go out for a walk to stretch our legs and get some fresh air, something we always did at home on Sundays after lunch, in the beautiful countryside around my home village. You cannot take the country girl out of me.

Nor forget to celebrate lunch.

Every day.

Watercress and orange salad
with cumin-flavored vinaigrette and pistachios

Plated like a carpaccio, this salad offers a rainbow of colors so pretty that it is sure to grab your attention. The salad has refreshing accents of citrus and pepper—lent by the Sichuan pepper with its unique aroma and slight lemony overtones—balanced by a pistachio vinaigrette that's piquant. It's truly a fantastic salad to start a meal.

To prepare the vinaigrette: In a bowl, combine the ingredients in this order: sea salt, Sichuan pepper, cumin, and vinegar. Add the shallot and leave to sit for 20 minutes so that the flavors blend. Pour in the olive and pistachio oils and whisk to emulsify. Add the parsley and set aside.

To prepare the salad: With a sharp serrated knife, peel the skin and pith from the oranges. Thinly slice the fruit; set aside.

In a large bowl, gently toss the radishes, avocado, cheese, and watercress. Add the vinaigrette and toss gently. Take 4 salad plates and arranges the slices of oranges on top, alternating between blood orange and regular orange, to create a nice pattern of colors. Place the watercress salad in the middle. Top with the pistachios and serve.

Serves 4

For the vinaigrette:

Sea salt

Sichuan pepper (ground in a pepper mill)

½ teaspoon ground cumin

1 tablespoon red wine vinegar

1 small shallot, finely chopped

2 tablespoons olive oil

1 tablespoon pistachio oil

1 tablespoon finely chopped flat-leaf parsley

For the salad:

4 regular oranges

4 blood oranges

8 pink radishes, thinly sliced (use a mandoline if you have one)

1 ripe avocado, peeled, pitted, diced, and drizzled with lemon juice to prevent discoloration

2 oz (70 g) feta cheese, crumbled

2 cups (60 g; 2 oz) watercress leaves

1 oz (30 g) shelled unsalted green pistachios, coarsely chopped

Coriander-flavored carrot and zucchini tartlets

with manchego cheese

Makes six 4 ½-inch tartlets

You will need: six 4 ½-inch tartlet molds and six 1 ½-inch ring molds

Brown rice, quinoa, and buckwheat crust (see Basic Recipes, page 22)

For the egg batter:
3 large eggs, lightly beaten
2 tablespoons chopped cilantro
5 tablespoons *crème fraîche* or heavy cream
Sea salt and pepper

3 tablespoons olive oil
2 thyme twigs
1 ½ teaspoons ground coriander
2 packed cups finely grated carrots
Sea salt and pepper
1 small yellow or green zucchini, finely grated
4 oz (120 g) *manchego* cheese, thinly sliced
3 oz (90 g) soft fresh goat cheese, crumbled

It's interesting to watch how some foods end up in my kitchen. The first time I baked these tartlets, the zucchini accent happened by accident. I didn't have enough carrots and thought, "Well, I have a zucchini, *alors, pourquoi pas?* (so, why not?)" I found the tartlets so tasty and pretty that I decided to make the dish regular in my repertoire whenever friends stay for lunch. I find that finely grating the vegetables really enhances the taste.

Preheat the oven to 400°F (200°C).

Roll and cut the dough to fit inside the tartlet molds. Arrange the dough inside each mold and using a fork, make small holes at the bottom. Prebake for 15 minutes (see Basic Cooking Techniques, page 27, for instructions). Remove the parchment paper and weights and set aside.

In a bowl, beat the eggs with the cilantro and *crème fraîche.* Season with sea salt and pepper and set aside.

In a frying pan, heat 2 tablespoons of the oil over medium heat. Add the thyme and 1 teaspoon of the coriander and cook for 1 minute, or until fragrant. Add the carrots and cook for 1 minute, stirring. Season with salt and pepper, cover, reduce the heat to low, and cook for 5 more minutes, or until the carrots are soft. Discard the thyme and transfer the carrots to a clean bowl; let cool.

In the same pan, heat the remaining 1 tablespoon oil over medium heat. Add the remaining ½ teaspoon coriander. Cook for 1 minute, then add the zucchini. Cook for 3 minutes, or until the zucchini is soft. Transfer to a small bowl and let cool. Add three-quarters of the egg batter to the carrots and mix well.

Add the rest of the egg batter to the zucchini and mix well.

Garnish the bottom of each tartlet with slices of *manchego* cheese. Place a 1 ½-inch ring mold in the middle of each tartlet and add the carrot mixture on the outside and the zucchini on the inside. Top the tartlets with goat cheese crumbles.

Place the tartlets in the oven and bake for 25 to 30 minutes, until the top is golden. Let cool for 5 minutes before serving. Enjoy with a salad.

Verrine nordique

with fingerling potato, smoked salmon, and cucumber in lemony yogurt sauce

I am always hungry when my mother prepares *une assiette nordique* (literally meaning a Norwegian plate). It's a dish she improvised one day before it became a classic in her repertoire, and one that I always crave when I visit. She makes sure to choose the best fingerling potatoes she can find, and once cooked, slices them in half. She arranges them on each dinner plate with slices of smoked salmon, lettuce, tomatoes, and slices of avocado. The salad comes with a *sauce au fromage blanc* (a soft fresh cheese similar to yogurt in texture) prepared with lemon juice, chives, shallot, and olive oil. With my own touches, my mother's exquisite salad inspired these uncomplicated yet delicious *verrines*. They have me dreaming of traveling to Norway.

Makes 4 verrines

1 small English cucumber, peeled and thinly sliced (use a mandoline if you have one)

Coarse sea salt

8 fingerling potatoes

4 slices of good-quality smoked salmon, folded or sliced in long sticks

Fish roe, to serve

For the sauce:

14 oz (400 g) whole milk Greek yogurt

3 tablespoons lemon juice

1 tablespoon chopped chives, plus more to serve

1 tablespoon chopped flat-leaf parsley

½ teaspoon peeled and finely grated fresh horseradish

1 small shallot, finely chopped

Sea salt

Crushed red peppercorns

2 tablespoons hazelnut oil or olive oil

Place the cucumber slices in a colander and sprinkle them with coarse sea salt. Let them rest for 1 hour for the water to release. In the meantime, steam the potatoes until cooked through, about 15 minutes. When they're cool enough to handle, peel and cut them widthwise into ½-inch slices.

To prepare the sauce: In a bowl, whisk the yogurt, lemon juice, fresh herbs, horseradish, and shallot. Season with sea salt and crushed red peppercorns and add the oil; whisk and set aside.

Take 4 small glasses and layer the ingredients in this order: slices of potatoes, yogurt sauce, slices of cucumber, yogurt sauce, and slices of potatoes. Finish with a slice of smoked salmon, and when ready to serve, top with fish roe and chopped chives.

A verrine *is a glass with layers of food neatly arranged inside. Verrines are similar to a parfait, except that they can be savory or sweet, cold or warm, sophisticated or casual, and typically served to start or finish a meal.*

Asian-style chicken and rice noodle salad

Serves 4

1 tablespoon safflower oil
1 chicken breast (about 200 g;
    7 oz)
Sea salt and pepper
10 ½ oz (300 g) wide rice
    noodles
½ English cucumber, peeled and
    thinly sliced
1 small fennel bulb, greens trimmed
    off, core removed, and thinly
    sliced (use a mandoline if you
    have one)
½ orange pepper, seeds and white
    membranes removed, thinly
    sliced
1 small red onion, thinly sliced (use a
    mandoline if you have one)
4 handfuls of arugula
2 tablespoons coarsely chopped Thai
    basil
20 mint leaves, chopped
Crushed red peppercorns, to serve

For the sauce:
1-inch piece fresh ginger, peeled and
    finely grated
1 garlic clove, minced
3 tablespoons fish sauce
Juice of 3 small limes
4 tablespoons sesame oil

It was when I lived in New Zealand with my friends Sandra and Keith that my understanding of Asian cooking broadened. The only thing that matches Sandra's love of *crème brûlée* is her passion for Thai food, so we ate Thai food frequently, which, to my delight, introduced me to the wonderful world of rice noodles. Wide rice noodles are best if purchased fresh—from an Asian grocery store—but if you cannot find them, dry ones work just as well. I like to add them to vegetable stir-fries, Asian-style soups, and salads, like this refreshing cold salad—the perfect meal for a hot summer day.

In a frying pan, heat the safflower oil over medium-high heat. Add the chicken breast and cook on each side for a few minutes, until cooked through. Season with sea salt and pepper, remove from the heat, and slice the chicken into ½-inch pieces; set aside.

If using dry rice noodles, soak them in boiling water for 10 minutes, drain, and set aside. If they are fresh, use them as suggested in the instructions on the package (I typically boil them for a shorter time).

To prepare the sauce: In a bowl, whisk together all the ingredients until the sauce emulsifies.

In another large bowl, combine the noodles, chicken, cucumber, fennel, orange pepper, red onion, arugula, basil, and mint leaves. Pour the sauce over and toss gently. Sprinkle with red peppercorns and adjust the seasoning, if necessary, with more sea salt and pepper, lime juice, sesame oil, or fish sauce. Divide among 4 bowls.

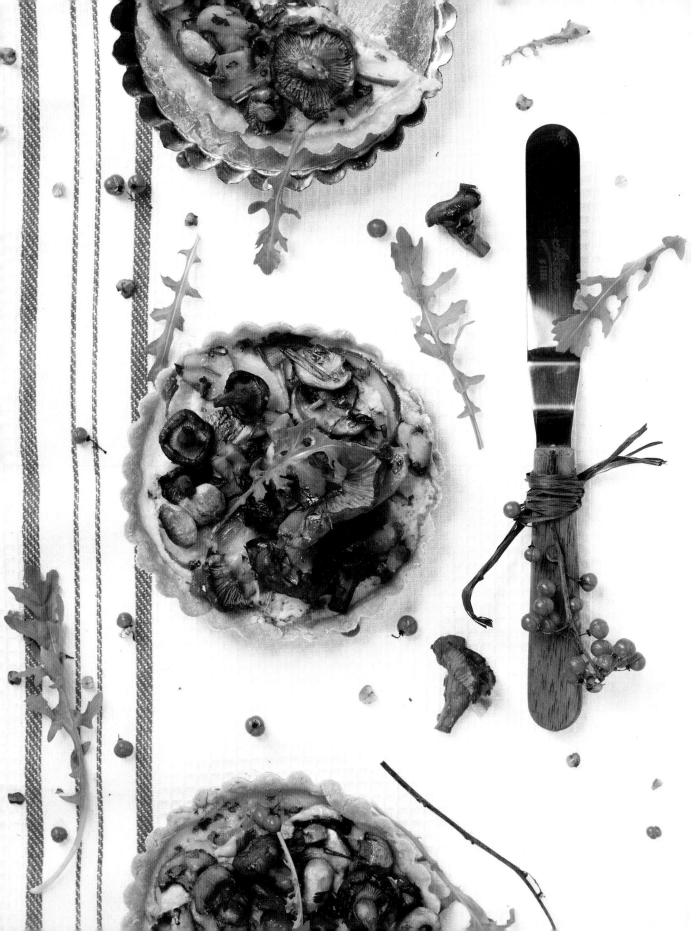

Mushroom and potato tartlets

Chanterelle mushrooms come out in late summer and early fall, and last for only a brief period of time. They're delicate in taste, original in shape, and a true highlight for any mushroom lover—like me. This tartlet recipe suggests using them with cremini mushrooms, but it's only because chanterelles can be fairly expensive—if your budget allows, use them alone—the flavor will be spectacular. Also, if you don't like blue cheese, substitute fresh goat cheese for a slightly more mellow taste.

Preheat the oven to 350°F (180°C).

Roll and cut the dough to fit inside the tartlet molds. Arrange the dough inside each mold and using a fork, make small holes at the bottom. Prebake for 10 minutes (see Basic Cooking Techniques, page 27, for instructions). Remove the parchment paper and weights and set aside.

Steam the potatoes until cooked through, 15 to 20 minutes, depending on their size. When they are cool enough to handle, peel them and cut them in ½-inch slices; set aside.

Clean the mushrooms—remove the dirt if necessary and wipe them with a damp paper towel—and slice them.

In a frying pan, heat the oil over medium heat. Add the leek and shallot and sauté for 2 to 3 minutes, stirring, without browning. Add the garlic and continue to cook for 1 minute. Add the mushrooms and season with sea salt and pepper. Cook for 5 to 6 minutes, stirring occasionally, until the mushrooms are soft and the liquid is evaporated. Transfer to a bowl and toss in 1 tablespoon of the parsley; set aside.

In a bowl, beat the eggs with the *crème fraîche*. Season with sea salt and pepper and stir in the remaining 1 tablespoon parsley.

Divide this egg batter among the crusts and arrange the potato slices on top. Place the tartlets in the oven and bake for 10 minutes. Remove from the oven and top with the crumbled cheese and the mushrooms. Return to the oven and bake for an additional 15 minutes. Serve warm with a green salad on the side.

Makes four 4 tartlets

You will need: four 4 ½-inch tartlet molds

Sweet rice, quinoa, and amaranth crust (see Basic Recipes, page 23)

4 small or 2 medium red potatoes

14 oz (400 g) mixed mushrooms (chanterelles and cremini, or one of the two)

2 tablespoons olive oil

1 small leek, white part only, diced

1 shallot, finely chopped

1 garlic clove, minced

Sea salt and pepper

2 tablespoons chopped flat-leaf parsley

2 small eggs

4 tablespoons *crème fraîche*

2 oz (60 g) Danish blue cheese or fresh goat cheese, crumbled

Caramelized cherry tomato, zucchini, and goat cheese clafoutis

Serves 4

You will need: a 10-inch
baking dish

3 tablespoons olive oil, plus more for
    the dish and zucchini

1 red onion, thinly sliced

Leaves from 2 thyme twigs, finely
    chopped

1 bay leaf

2 garlic cloves, minced

1 pound 2 oz (500 g) medium cherry
    tomatoes

1 tablespoon balsamic vinegar

1 teaspoon light Muscovado sugar

1 medium zucchini, thinly sliced
    lengthwise (use a mandoline if
    you have one)

⅓ cup (40 g; 1½ oz) cornstarch

½ cup (120 ml) whole milk

3 large eggs

½ cup (120 ml) heavy cream

1 oz (30 g) grated pecorino or Comté
    cheese

5 to 6 basil leaves, coarsely chopped

Sea salt and pepper

2 oz (60 g) fresh goat cheese, crum-
    bled

If you've traveled to France or visited my Web site before, you'll undoubtedly have seen the word *clafoutis*. It's a word that should be written in all caps, with glitter, to jump out at you—yes, I am a *clafoutis* lover. Traditionally, *clafoutis* is a custardlike French dessert made by baking cherries in an egg batter—I've given you a recipe for this in the Dessert section (page 248)—but this dish happily welcomes many variants, including savory ones like this cherry tomato and zucchini *clafoutis*. Choose ripe cherry tomatoes that are sweet and full of character for a spectacular summery dish, perfect for lunch enjoyed under the umbrella outside.

Preheat the oven to 400°F (200°C); brush a 10-inch baking dish with oil and set aside.

In a frying pan, heat 2 tablespoons of the oil over medium heat. Add the onion and thyme and cook, without browning, for 4 minutes, stirring, until fragrant and the onion has softened. Add the bay leaf and garlic and cook for 1 more minute. Add the tomatoes and cook for 2 more minutes, stirring gently, then add the vinegar and sugar. Continue to cook for 3 more minutes. Discard the thyme and bay leaf; set aside.

In the same pan, heat the remaining 1 tablespoon oil. Arrange the zucchini slices at the bottom (you might need to do this in a few batches) and cook for 30 seconds on each side, adding more oil as needed. Remove from the heat and set aside.

In a bowl, beat the cornstarch into the milk. In another bowl, beat the eggs. Mix the diluted cornstarch, the heavy cream, and grated cheese into the eggs. Add the basil, season with sea salt and pepper, and mix well.

Arrange the vegetables at the bottom of the dish. Pour the egg batter in and top with the crumbled goat cheese.

Place the *clafoutis* in the oven and bake for 30 minutes, or until the egg flan is set and the top is golden in color. Serve with a green salad.

Spicy spaghetti

with wilted arugula, lime, basil, and prosciutto

As many people do, when Philip and I crave a comforting, quick-to-prepare meal, we often think *spaghetti*. I improvise on how to dress the pasta with whatever I find in the fridge. The day I dug out a box of arugula, tomatoes, a few limes, and fresh herbs—staple foods I keep handy—I created this dish, and ever since then it's become a regular meal in our house. And if I happen to have some prosciutto on hand—pretty much all the time, especially if Philip went grocery shopping—we top our plates with that too. Scrumptious!

Blanch the tomatoes in salted boiling water for 1 minute. Rinse them under cold water, then peel, core, and dice them.

In a wok, heat 2 tablespoons of the oil over medium heat. Add the onion, garlic, lime zest, lemon thyme, and chile and cook for 3 to 4 minutes. Add the tomatoes, sugar, and bay leaf and season with sea salt and pepper. Reduce the heat to medium-low and cook for about 15 minutes, stirring occasionally, until the tomatoes have softened.

In the meantime, cook the spaghetti following the instructions on the package. Transfer to a bowl and add the remaining 2 tablespoons oil.

Add the pasta and arugula to the wok. Remove from the heat and toss until the arugula is wilted from the heat of the spaghetti. Discard the bay leaf and lemon thyme and add the lime juice and basil. Check the seasoning for more sea salt if necessary—although the Parmesan will bring salt. Serve with plenty of grated Parmesan cheese and prosciutto slices on top.

Serves 4

4 large ripe tomatoes

Sea salt and pepper

4 tablespoons olive oil

1 medium red onion, thinly sliced

4 garlic cloves, finely chopped

Zest and juice of 1 large organic lime

3 lemon thyme twigs

1 small habanero chile, seeds removed and diced

2 teaspoons light Muscovado sugar

1 bay leaf

12 oz (340 g) spaghetti

4 packed cups (100 g; 3 ½ oz) arugula

2 heaping tablespoons roughly chopped basil

Finely grated Parmesan cheese, to taste

4 prosciutto slices, or more if you like, to serve

Dinners to Inspire

Casual Dinners with Friends   167

Sophisticated and Elegant Dinners   189

"Vous resterez bien pour diner?" ("You'll stay for dinner?") my grandmother asked in a coarse voice from across the dining table. Her impeccable-looking silver gray hair made her beautiful light blue eyes stand out even more. Her head was hunched over a bag of dirty-looking potatoes picked in the garden that she was peeling and slicing thick, to make roasted potatoes for dinner. They're still to this day the best roasted potatoes I've ever eaten, always cooked to perfection with a crisp shining golden brown skin that reveals a creamy buttery flesh inside.

"Oh oui, s'il te plait!" ("Yes, please!") my brother Benoit and I replied enthusiastically without leaving a second for my mother to decide.

We loved to stay at my grandmother's for dinner; we wanted to taste her potatoes, the pork *saucisson* (sausage), *pâté de lapin* (rabbit pâté), and *jambon fumé* (smoked ham) she had made and that, we knew, she was going to take out from her pantry if we stayed. Invariably, she asked me to run to the back garden to pick a green salad to go along with our simple meal.

I remember my grandmother for her natural cooking skills too. My father's parents both lived on a farm, and in their kitchen, there was a long farm table that filled every day with

expected—or unexpected—guests for lunch or dinner. She never really knew how many mouths she would have to feed, but that never seemed to bother her. She had this *"je-ne-sais-quoi"* talent that made her deal with it, no matter what, even if that meant that thirty hungry mouths were gathered around the table, like every August 15th when we celebrated *la Sainte Marie*. I was fascinated by her ease at doing it so well each time.

My mother has the same ease in the kitchen, in fact, and I've taken it for granted that dinner should naturally be prepared at home.

The year of my seventeenth birthday, when I went to college and lived alone in a small studio apartment in Metz, France, I cooked dinner every night. My kitchen was extremely tiny and awkward, the size of what you find at the back of a small airplane. It had an electric two-plate stove that I hated when I first moved in, but that I learned to handle. My desire to cook was strong. My desire to eat like I had at home was even stronger. So I took the skills learned by my mother's side and developed them further on my own. And found out quickly that my friends liked to stay for dinner, and that I enjoyed cooking for them.

I know that I am fortunate. There isn't a better school than watching your grandmother and mother magically transform raw foods into spectacular meals, using fresh produce and vegetables they grow in the garden. I learned that summer is for canning and making preserves when the fruit and vegetables are ripe and plentiful, and that during winter, we eat the preserves we've made. And that the best meals that you'll ever eat are the ones that you prepare with your heart and you share.

I hope that I will pass the same love for homemade foods on to my sweet daughter, Lulu, just as my mother and grandmother did with me.

THE PARTY WITH SMALL BITES

I really like to throw a party. You know, the kind of joyful evening when you wear one of your over-the-top dresses and pretty shoes; the house is lively with the conversations and laughter of your friends; your favorite music is playing in the background; there are bottles of good wine and champagne—and there are countless plates of cute finger foods.

For days I'll think about the party, daydreaming and rehearsing each detail in my head. Driving myself crazy in the process too, because that's simply my nature. I imagine colorful bunches of freshly cut flowers to make the house smell fresh like spring, and I picture pretty tablecloths with assorted napkins and my favorite glasses on the table. And then, I imagine *le plat de résistance* (the centerpiece): the food! Because that's what I like to do the best.

Friends are important, mind you, but oh the foods! Who will not remember a party for its food and wine? Assuredly, the food served will turn an average party into a memorable one.

Over the years that we've lived together, Philip and I have had a fair amount of parties at home. We like to organize them together and use our skills where they fit best: While he chooses the wine and tidies and cleans the mess I inevitably leave behind

in the kitchen—he doesn't even complain that I make too much of it!—I make the house look pretty and prepare delicious finger foods.

I prepare these foods the way I do crafts—with close attention to details, colors, and shapes, whether they are simple or more intricate. They will be small in size so that our guests can easily walk around the room holding a glass in one hand and a small plate in the other. They will be foods that produce a burst of flavors in one bite and that you can eat as many of as you like without ever feeling it's too many.

Of course, at our parties, we eat more than we should and drink more than is reasonable. We dance and play silly games with the last guests around. When everyone is gone, Philip and I take our shoes off and lay on the floor. He'll whisper something like *That was nice!* in my ear.

"Yes!" I'd agree, feeling tired happy. "When are we having another one?"

Cumin and parsley-flavored cheese gougères

The time I drove to the Champagne area of France to pick grapes, I met Madame Jolly, the mother of the vineyard owner. She was a chatty and lively woman of seventy-eight years of age, always dressed impeccably. She also made the best *gougères*, introducing me to the art of serving these cheese-flavored puffs to accompany a glass of champagne. We enjoyed spending time together in the kitchen, where she'd tell me stories about her favorite recipes. And to my delight, I returned home with her *gougère* recipe scribbled in her own handwriting on a piece of paper. Over the years I've experimented with it, always successfully, and cannot help think about her whenever I bake my own variant.

Note: If you prefer to make a more traditional, and non-gluten-free gougère, you can substitute 1 cup all-purpose flour for the quinoa flour and cornstarch.

Makes 18 gougères

You will need: a pastry bag fitted with a wide plain tip

½ cup (120 ml) whole milk
½ cup (120 ml) water
½ teaspoon sea salt
Pinch of pepper
6 tablespoons (85 g; 3 oz) unsalted butter, diced
½ cup plus 1 tablespoon (75 g; 2 ½ oz) quinoa flour
⅓ cup cornstarch (40 g; 1 ½ oz)
4 large eggs
5 ½ oz (150 g) grated cheese, such as Comté, Beaufort, cheddar, Emmentaler, or Gruyère
1 tablespoon chopped flat-leaf parsley
1 tablespoon cumin seeds

Make sure to have all the ingredients ready before you begin, as it is important to work quickly once you start.

Preheat the oven to 420°F (215°C). Prepare 2 baking sheets by covering them with parchment paper; set aside.

In a pot, combine the milk, water, sea salt, and pepper with the butter and bring to a boil. Once the milk reaches the boiling point, pour the flour and cornstarch into the pot and stir vigorously with a wooden spoon until the mixture pulls away from the sides of the pot.

Remove from the heat and let the dough rest for 2 minutes. Add the eggs, one at a time, stirring quickly and waiting for the first egg to be incorporated before adding the next. The dough will be smooth and elastic.

Add three-quarters of the grated cheese and the parsley, and stir until the ingredients are incorporated. Scrape the dough into a pastry bag fitted with a wide plain tip and pipe into 1 ½-inch mounds onto the baking sheets, with 2 inches between each. Top each puff with the rest of the cheese and the cumin seeds.

Place the *gougères* in the oven and bake for 10 minutes, then reduce the heat to 350°F (180°C). Bake for 10 to 15 more minutes, until the *gougères* are golden brown in color. Remove from the oven and let cool slightly before eating. If you make them ahead of time, warm them for 5 minutes in the oven at 350°F (180°C) before serving.

Belgian endive leaves

with Roquefort, grapes, and radishes dressed in pistachio vinaigrette

When used as finger food, Belgian endive leaves make eye-catching bite-size edible spoons. The filling—tiny cubes of Roquefort, radishes, and grapes—is dressed in a pistachio vinaigrette that blends harmoniously with the bitter taste of the salad. In fact, whenever I decide to serve them, the most difficult part of the preparation is refraining from eating them. If you've never used pistachio oil before, once you taste it here you'll wonder why you've never indulged.

To prepare the vinaigrette: In a small bowl, combine the ingredients in the order listed. Whisk to emulsify; set aside.

Separate the endive leaves, choose the best-looking ones (they shouldn't be too big), and wash them. Pat them dry with a clean kitchen towel and place them on a large serving plate.

Combine the pistachios, grapes, and radishes in a bowl 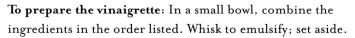Add the cheese crumbles and toss gently. Season with the vinaigrette.

Place a heaping teaspoon of this mixture inside each endive leaf and top with a sprinkle of pistachios and a piece of dill. It's a good idea to have an extra endive handy, should you prefer the shape of the leaves or if you need more. You'll be happy to snack on whatever is left!

Makes about 15 pieces

For the pistachio vinaigrette:

Sea salt and pepper

1 garlic clove, minced

1 tablespoon aged balsamic vinegar

2 tablespoons pistachio oil

1 tablespoon canola oil

For the finger food:

2 Belgian endives

2 tablespoons shelled unsalted green pistachios, coarsely chopped

¾ cup (150 g; 5 ¼ oz) red grapes, cut into ¼-inch pieces

6 pink radishes, cut into ¼-inch pieces

3 oz (90 g) Roquefort cheese, crumbled

Dill, to decorate

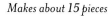

Potato nests filled with gingered crab

Makes 18 to 20 nests

1 large (225 g; 8 oz) baking potato or
   sweet potato, peeled and finely
   grated
1 large egg, lightly beaten
½ teaspoon freshly grated nutmeg
1 tablespoon chopped flat-leaf
   parsley
Sea salt
Crushed red or black peppercorns
3 tablespoons unsalted butter,
   melted
½ organic green apple, cored and
   diced
1 tablespoon lime juice
½ cup (100 g; 3 ½ oz) cooked fresh
   crabmeat
1 tablespoon olive oil
1 tablespoon chopped cilantro
1 scallion, finely chopped
½ tablespoon chopped chives, plus a
   few sprigs to serve
Crème fraîche, to serve
2 tablespoons pomegranate seeds,
   to serve
Fleur de sel, to serve

These potato nests are among the cutest finger foods I enjoy
preparing. Don't be fooled by their appearance—they might
look complicated, but in reality they are very simple to make.
And the result is a delectable adventure with every bite.

Preheat the oven to 420°F (215°C). Oil a mini muffin pan or
two with cooking spray; set aside.

In a bowl, beat the grated potato with the egg and nutmeg.
Add the parsley and season with sea salt and crushed red peppercorns. Take a small amount of the grated potatoes in your
hands and squeeze out the excess liquid. Press this into the bottom of each muffin hole in the shape of a nest; repeat with the
remaining grated potatoes. Add ½ teaspoon of melted butter to
each nest.

Place in the oven and bake for 25 minutes, or until the
potatoes are crisp and golden in color. Unmold the nests and
let cool on a rack.

In a bowl, gently toss the apple with the lime juice, crab, oil,
cilantro, scallion, and chives. Season with sea salt and pepper.
Using a teaspoon, spoon a small amount of filling inside each
potato nest. Add a dollop of *crème fraîche* and a few pomegranate seeds. Sprinkle with *fleur de sel* and decorate with a few chive
sprigs.

Buckwheat blini

with smoked salmon, apples, and crème fraîche

Cocktail *blini* are classic party food that never fails to please. I like to give mine more character by adding buckwheat flour to the batter and dressing them up with slices of smoked salmon and apple, and finishing them with a dollop of *crème fraîche*. I particularly like the contrast of textures and flavors, as each bite offers crunch and smoothness as well as sweet and savory tastes. If you need to save time, prepare the blini ahead of time and freeze them. When you want to use them, reheat them in an oven at 350°F (180°C) for 5 to 10 minutes to bring them back to room temperature.

Makes twenty to twenty-two 3-inch blini

You will need: a fluted 2 ½-inch cookie cutter

For the *blini*:

⅔ cup (160 ml) whole milk

⅓ cup (80 ml) buttermilk, at room temperature

⅓ cup (50 g; 1 ¾ oz) buckwheat flour

⅓ cup (40 g; 1 ½ oz) millet flour

⅓ cup (40 g; 1 ½ oz) quinoa flour

2 tablespoons cornstarch

1 teaspoon active dry yeast

¼ teaspoon sea salt

2 large eggs, separated, at room temperature

Safflower oil, for cooking

To serve:

10 slices of smoked salmon, cut in half

Crème fraîche, to serve

1 large green apple, cored and thinly sliced, drizzled with lemon juice

Chopped dill, to serve

In a pot, heat the milk until lukewarm. Stir in the buttermilk; set aside.

In a bowl, combine the flours with the cornstarch, yeast, and sea salt. Stir in the milk mixture, then the egg yolks. Mix until the batter is smooth. Cover the bowl with a clean kitchen towel and place it in a warm spot where you are sure there is no draft. Let the batter rise for about an hour, until bubbles form at the surface.

In another bowl, beat the egg whites until soft peaks form, then fold them into the batter. Cover with the towel again and let the batter rest in a warm area for 1 hour.

In a frying pan, heat the oil over medium heat. Drop 2 tablespoons of batter in for each *blini*, repeating for as many as your pan can hold. Cook each *blini* until bubbles form at the surface (it takes between 1 and 2 minutes), and then flip the *blini* on the other side. Cook for 1 more minute; set aside. Add more oil to the pan as needed.

Once the *blini* are cooked, use a fluted 2 ½-inch cookie cutter to cut the *blini* to give them uniform pretty shapes.

To serve, top each *blini* with a folded slice of smoked salmon, a dollop of *crème fraîche*, a slice of green apple, and chopped dill.

Crustless mini quiches
with sweet marinated cucumber and mint

> A lighter variant of a quiche is to bake one without a crust. You will love to have this recipe handy for the times when you need a finger food that's quick to prepare and pretty to serve with a drink to a crowd of friends.

Makes 32 mini quiches

6 large eggs

Sea salt and pepper

1 teaspoon ground cumin

⅔ cup (160 ml) heavy cream

⅔ cup finely grated Parmesan cheese

1 tablespoon finely chopped dill

For the topping:

1 cup thinly sliced cucumber (use a mandoline if you have one) (about ¼ long English cucumber)

Sea salt

5 tablespoons white rice vinegar

1 ½ tablepoons blond cane sugar

1 teaspoon finely chopped mint

1 teaspoon finely chopped dill

Crème fraîche, to serve

Pink fish roe, to serve

Mint leaves, to serve

Preheat the oven to 350°F (180°C). Oil mini muffin pans with cooking spray; set aside.

In a bowl, beat the eggs with a pinch of sea salt and pepper. Add the cumin and continue to mix. Stir in the heavy cream, Parmesan, and dill, and mix until smooth.

Fill the muffin pans three-quarters of the way full, place in the oven, and bake for about 15 minutes, until puffed up and lightly browned. Note that the quiches will deflate once removed from the oven, and that's normal. Unmold and let cool on a rack.

Place the cucumber in a colander and sprinkle it with 1 teaspoon sea salt. Let rest for 30 minutes so that the cucumber releases its water. Drain and transfer to a bowl. In a small bowl, whisk the vinegar with the sugar until it's dissolved. Add the mint and dill and mix well. Pour this dressing over the cucumber and toss gently. Cover and refrigerate for at least 1 hour, or until ready to use.

When ready to serve, arrange the mini quiches on a serving plate. Add a few slices of cucumber on each and a small dollop of *crème fraîche.* Finish with a few fish roe eggs and a small leaf of mint.

DINNERS FOR
GETAWAY WEEKENDS

"Comment est équipée la cuisine?" ("How equipped is the kitchen?") I asked my mother on the phone. I was calling her from Zurich as Philip and I were waiting for our connecting flight to Geneva.

My parents had rented a quaint chalet in Combloux, a small village near Mont Blanc in the French Alps, where the whole family was gathering for Christmas. *Oh,* how impatient I felt! To feel the crisp mountain air on my cheeks. To ski, walk, share conversations, cook, and eat with my family.

"Pas mal" ("Not bad"), she replied. *"On se débrouillera."* ("We'll manage.")

And in fact, we managed well.

Every morning, my father volunteered to walk to the village bakery to buy fresh *baguettes à l'ancienne* and brioche. Since he doesn't cook, *absolument rien* (nothing at all), he wanted to be in charge of that. And we were glad, as it meant that the bread would still be warm when we ate it—and we could sleep in longer.

Breakfast was a feast. We started with fruit, cheese, ham, soft-boiled eggs, granola, yogurt, bread, and jam to boost our energy. I've noticed that whenever we go skiing—which is an annual family tradition—my morning appetite is always enormous, and breakfast already feels like lunch. We'd spend the day snowshoeing or on the ski slopes, and at around 4:30 p.m., we'd make a daily stop at the *crêperie* stand to buy a *crêpe* each. That never spoiled dinner.

In the evening, we'd take turns cooking, always hungry for homey nourishing foods!

One night, I prepared a radicchio risotto with a few heads of the pretty red vegetable we'd bought at the local *marché* (outdoor produce market). The rice tasted rich and creamy, and the dish felt earthy and yet sophisticated too. And so tasty that everyone asked for seconds. Another night, it was my brother who cooked and made a spectacular chicken *tajine berbère,* the way he had learned when he traveled to Morocco. I can still picture him as he walked to the table holding the steaming hot *tajine* dish in his hands. He was proud—but in his usual manner didn't show it—to see that everyone gobbled down the whole thing quietly within minutes, using pieces of bread to clean up the last bit of juice on the plates. As for my mother, she prepared a *boeuf aux carottes,* a dish she used to make on Sundays during the winter when I was growing up—my brother and I loved it because the next day she'd often use the leftovers to prepare a *hachis parmentier,* the French equivalent of a shepherd's pie.

My sister-in-law cooked fresh pasta with vegetables, and I baked cinnamon muffins that we enjoyed as a day snack. On Christmas day, I baked chocolate mousse and raspberry cakes, using the ring molds and plastic cake wraps I had packed in my luggage along with measuring cups. Philip had looked at me funny as he watched me slip my cooking material inside my bag. *"Mais qu'est-ce que tu fais avec ça dans ta valise?"* ("What are you doing with *this* in your suitcase?") he had exclaimed. But once I had explained my reason, he stopped inquiring. He smiled. And then he kissed me, looking forward, I was sure, to the moment when I would bring dessert to the dining table.

We put a lot of ourselves into our meals. They brought us together around the table every day, allowing each of us to share a bit of ourselves. And that week, like the many others Philip and I have spent away, with family and friends, felt precious. We were happy to share stories . . . and build memories around food.

Eggplant stuffed with white sweet potato

Stuffing eggplants is one of my preferred ways to eat these pretty vegetables. During the summer when I was writing this cookbook, I made this dish almost every week, adding or changing one ingredient each time. The day I decided to add white sweet potato to the stuffing, I knew that I had found *my* recipe and never wanted to change it again.

Serves 4

4 Italian eggplants

Sea salt

4 tablespoons olive oil

1 red onion, finely chopped

1 celery stalk, diced

1 tablespoon ground coriander

½ tablespoon chopped lemon thyme

Pinch of red chile flakes

3 garlic cloves, minced

1 tablespoon double-concentrated tomato paste

2 large tomatoes, blanched, peeled, seeded, and diced

1 large carrot, peeled and finely grated

1 white or regular sweet potato, peeled and diced

1 bay leaf

4 oz (120 g) Emmentaler cheese, grated

1 tablespoon chopped cilantro

Slice each eggplant in half. Using a grapefruit spoon or teaspoon, carefully scoop out the flesh, making sure to keep the outer skin of the eggplants intact. Transfer the flesh to a board and chop; set aside. Sprinkle the inside of the eggplants with sea salt and turn them over; leave for 30 minutes.

In a sauté pan, heat 2 tablespoons of the oil over medium heat. Add the onion, celery, ground coriander, lemon thyme, and chile flakes. Cook, without browning, for 2 to 3 minutes, stirring occasionally. Add the garlic, tomato paste, and tomatoes and continue to cook for 4 minutes, stirring. Add the carrot, sweet potato, eggplant flesh, and bay leaf, and season with sea salt. Cover and simmer for about 25 minutes, stirring occasionally, until the vegetables are soft. Discard the bay leaf. Stir in three-quarters of the cheese and the cilantro.

Preheat the oven to 400°F (200°C).

Stuff the eggplant skins with the cooked vegetables and sprinkle with the rest of the cheese. Place the stuffed eggplants in an oven dish and drizzle with the remaining 2 tablespoons oil. Pour a little water in the bottom of the dish and bake for 45 to 50 minutes, until nicely colored on top. I like to serve this dish with fresh pasta and salad.

Italian eggplants are thinner and more elongated than regular eggplants. I find that their flesh is also more tender and tastier than the common variety. It's a lovely choice when you want to stuff eggplants, as they are the perfect serving size.

Radicchio risotto

Serves 4

4 tablespoons olive oil, plus more to
    serve

1 red onion, thinly sliced

3 garlic cloves, minced

1 medium head radicchio, thinly
    sliced (300 g; 10 ½ oz; 4 to 5
    packed cups)

½ cup (120 ml) plus ⅓ cup
    (80 ml) red wine (like a Côtes
    du Rhône)

1 bay leaf

Sea salt and pepper

2 tablespoons balsamic vinegar

4 ½ cups (1 liter 60 ml) chicken
    broth, or more as needed

1 tablespoon (14 g; ½ oz) unsalted
    butter

4 thyme twigs

1 ½ cups (300 g; 10 ½ oz) carnaroli
    rice, or another risotto rice such
    as Vialone Nano or Arborio

1 ½ oz (40 g) pecorino or Parmesan
    cheese, finely grated, plus more
    to serve

3 tablespoons *crème fraîche* or
    mascarpone cheese

1 tablespoon chopped flat-leaf
    parsley

Radicchio has a deep purple color that makes the dishes that it's added to look dramatic and stunning. Its subtle bitter taste mellows once it's cooked, so it develops wonderful flavors in a risotto like this one. This was the dish I made when we spent Christmas with my family in Combloux, France, and that everyone ate to the last piece of rice stuck at the bottom of the pot.

In a sauté pan, heat 2 tablespoons of the oil over medium heat. Add the onion and cook for 2 minutes, stirring, without browning, until soft. Add the garlic and cook for 1 more minute, or until fragrant. Add the radicchio and cook, stirring, for 4 minutes, until soft. Add ½ cup of the red wine and the bay leaf; season with sea salt and pepper and cook, uncovered, over medium heat until most of the liquid is evaporated, 7 to 8 minutes. Add the vinegar and cook for 2 more minutes. Remove from the heat and discard the bay leaf; set aside.

In a pot, heat the broth; keep warm. In a heavy pot, melt the butter over medium heat. Add the remaining 2 tablespoons oil, then add the thyme twigs. Cook for about 1 minute, until fragrant. Pour in the rice and coat, stirring, for 1 minute. Add the remaining ⅓ cup red wine and cook the rice, stirring, until all the liquid is absorbed. Add 1 cup of broth, reduce the heat to medium-low, and continue to cook, stirring constantly. Wait until all the liquid is absorbed to add more broth. When you've added three-quarters of the broth, stir in the warm radicchio. At this point, check how done the rice is, and add the rest of the broth as needed. The risotto should be creamy but stay slightly al dente.

Remove from the heat and stir in the pecorino cheese with the *crème fraîche* and parsley. Cover and let rest for 2 minutes. Serve with more grated cheese and drizzle each plate with 1 teaspoon of oil.

Marjoram-flavored ricotta and zucchini tart

"It's like having a beam of sunshine in your plate!" I said to Philip when I made this tart the first time. "It's full of zest too!" he responded, eating a slice.

When the season is right and the garden offers beautiful zucchini of all shapes and colors—from deep green to light green and yellow—you'll probably love this tart—with its sweet accents of marjoram, honey, and lime—as much as we do. It is bound to make you happy.

Preheat the oven to 400°F (200°C).

To prepare the crust, roll the dough and cut a circle slightly bigger than the mold. Arrange the dough inside the mold and, using a fork, make small holes at the bottom. Prebake for 10 minutes (see Basic Cooking Technique, page 27, for instructions); remove the parchment paper and weights and set aside.

In a bowl, beat the ricotta cheese with the herbs and lime zest. Stir in the oil and season with sea salt and pepper. Spread this mixture evenly over the crust. Arrange the slices of zucchini on top, alternating between green and yellow, and repeating until you run out of zucchini. Add the slices of cheese between the zucchini—you won't have as many slices of cheese as you have of zucchini, so place them evenly between the slices of zucchini. Drizzle with the honey and olive oil.

Place the tart in the oven and bake for 40 minutes, or until the cheese is melted and lightly colored. Remove the tart from the oven and let rest for 5 minutes before slicing. Serve with a salad.

Makes one 10-inch mold; serves 4

You will need: a 10-inch tart mold

Millet, amaranth, and brown rice crust (see Basic Recipes, page 23)

1 cup (200 g; 7 oz) whole milk ricotta cheese

1 tablespoon chopped marjoram

1 tablespoon chopped parsley

Finely grated zest of ½ organic lime

1 tablespoon olive oil, plus more to drizzle

Sea salt and pepper

1 small green zucchini, thinly sliced (use a mandoline if you have one)

1 small yellow zucchini, thinly sliced (use a mandoline if you have one)

3 oz (90 g) Swiss-type cheese (like Emmentaler or Beaufort if you can find it), thinly sliced

1 tablespoon honey

Three root vegetable gratin dauphinois

The chances of eating a *gratin dauphinois* when I visit my parents in France are high: It's a classic in my mother's cooking repertoire, and she is the one who taught me how to make it too. This creamy potato dish—so utterly French—is a wonderful accompaniment to any roasted meat, but Philip and I like it so much that we sometimes eat it as a meal in itself, with a tossed salad on the side. You can choose to use only potatoes, which is what goes into a traditional French *gratin dauphinois* (without cheese), but I like the complexity of flavors that other root vegetables, and a fruity cheese like Beaufort, add. For a more formal meal, I bake individual servings in small dishes so that each person can scrape up every single delicious bit found at the bottom of their dish.

Note: For a variation, substitute the Jerusalem artichokes with 1 large sweet potato, and the purple turnips with 5 or 6 medium pink turnips. It's the promise of a colorful gratin.

Serves 6

1 ½ cups (350 ml) whole milk

1 ½ cups (350 ml) heavy cream

5 sage leaves, chopped

5 thyme twigs

1 bay leaf

1 garlic clove sliced in half

Unsalted butter, for the dish

1 pound 12 oz (800 g) Yukon gold or
    russet potatoes
      (4 to 5 medium potatoes),
      peeled

9 oz (250 g) Jerusalem artichokes
    (about 10 small ones), peeled

9 oz (250 g) purple turnips

Sea salt and pepper

1 teaspoon freshly grated nutmeg

2 oz (60 g) grated Beaufort or
    Comté cheese

In a pot, combine the milk and heavy cream. Add the sage, thyme, and bay leaf and bring to a boil, making sure it doesn't overflow. Remove from the heat, cover, and leave to infuse for 1 hour; strain and set aside.

Preheat the oven to 400°F (200°C). Rub a 9-by-12-inch baking dish with half of the garlic clove. Butter the dish and slice the other half of the garlic. Place the slices in the bottom of the dish and set aside.

Using a mandoline or a sharp knife, cut all the vegetables into ¹/₁₆-inch slices. Layer the slices of vegetables tightly in the buttered dish following this order: potatoes, Jerusalem artichokes, potatoes, turnip, and potatoes again; repeat again until you run out of ingredients, seasoning each layer with sea salt and pepper. Reheat the milk-cream mixture until hot and pour over the vegetables—you should have enough to cover the vegetables. If necessary, press down on the vegetables with the back of a wooden spoon to make sure that they are covered with liquid so they stay moist. Top with the nutmeg and cheese.

Place the gratin in the oven and bake for 50 minutes to 1 hour, or until it's nicely browned on top and the liquid is absorbed.

Tagliatelle

with zucchini, lime, and Parmesan

Serves 4

Sea salt

12 oz (340 g) tagliatelle or
    spaghetti

4 tablespoons olive oil

1 pound (450 g) bay scallops, if using

1 red onion, thinly sliced

Finely grated zest and juice of
    1 organic lime

Pinch of red chile flakes

1 celery stalk, diced

4 garlic cloves, minced

2 zucchini, finely julienned (use a
    julienne peeler if you have one)

1 cup (90 g; 3 oz) freshly grated Par-
    mesan cheese, plus more for
    serving.

¼ cup chopped cilantro

Truffle oil, to serve

I prepared this tagliatelle dish when Philip and I went to Martha's Vineyard for our first vacation away with Lulu. She was only ten months old. I hadn't planned it but I cooked this dish spontaneously with what I had handy (without the scallops and truffle oil then). We enjoyed the flavors so much that this became lunch one day, and dinner the next night. The list of ingredients is minimal, but each stands out beautifully. Lightly sautéed scallops and truffle oil are a delightful addition for when you want to dress the dish up more.

Bring a large pot of water to a boil. Add a generous pinch of sea salt and cook the pasta according to the instructions on the package. Drain, transfer to a bowl, and gently toss with 1 tablespoon of the oil; cover to keep warm.

If using scallops, in a frying pan, heat 1 tablespoon of the remaining oil over medium heat. Add the scallops and cook them quickly, for barely 1 minute, stirring, until they firm up on the outside; transfer to a bowl and cover to keep warm.

In a wok, heat the remaining 2 tablespoons oil over medium heat. Add the red onion, lime zest, chile flakes, and celery stalk. Cook for 2 to 3 minutes, stirring, until the onion and celery soften. Add the garlic and continue to cook for 1 minute. Add the zucchini and cook for 1 minute more. At this point, add the spaghetti and the bay scallops to the wok and season with the lime juice. Toss gently and stir in the cheese and cilantro.

Serve in deep plates with a drizzle of truffle oil and more grated cheese to your liking.

Tomatoes stuffed with pork, mashed potatoes, olives, and sage

> The love affair I have with stuffed vegetables started with my mother's *tomates farcies* (stuffed tomatoes). She'd prepare her dish every week during the summer, when the tomatoes in her garden were plump and juicy. Invariably, her recipe—a filling made of ground beef, garlic, onion, and parsley into which she stirs an egg—was a hit. It's also the dish that inspired me to experiment with new ideas on how to stuff tomatoes. So that now, even when I prepare completely different variants on the same idea, it brings me back to the memory of her making *tomates farcies* in her kitchen.

Preheat the oven to 350°F (180°C).

Cut the top off of each tomato and set them aside for later. Using a teaspoon or small knife, scoop the flesh out of the tomatoes. Sprinkle inside the tomatoes with sea salt and turn them upside down, letting them rest for 30 minutes to release their water.

In the meantime, boil the potatoes in a pot of salted water for 15 minutes, until they are fork-tender. Using a ricer or food mill, mash them. Transfer to a bowl and add the ground pork, mascarpone, sage, parsley, olives, shallot, and three-quarters of the grated cheese. Season with sea salt and pepper and add 1 tablespoon of olive oil. Stuff the tomatoes with this filling. Top with the rest of the cheese and cover with the reserved tomato tops.

Arrange the tomatoes in a 9-by-12-inch oven dish and drizzle generously with oil. Add enough water to cover the bottom of the dish and bake the tomatoes for 35 to 40 minutes, until the tomatoes look juicy and cooked through.

Serves 4 (makes 12 tomatoes)

12 tomatoes

Sea salt

4 Yukon gold potatoes, peeled and diced

9 oz (250 g) ground pork

3 tablespoons mascarpone cheese or *crème fraîche*

6 sage leaves, chopped

1 tablespoon chopped flat-leaf parsley

8 kalamata olives, pitted and finely chopped

1 shallot, finely chopped

1 oz (30 g) finely grated Gruyère or Comté cheese

1 tablespoon olive oil, plus more for drizzling

Pepper

Eggplant, lamb, and winter squash crumble

Although the French didn't invent crumbles, they've welcomed the dish without any difficulty—and to top it off, they even imagined savory crumbles. The idea behind this dish is simple: take the concept of a traditional sweet crumble and replace the fruit with vegetables and meat, and the sugar with fresh herbs and cheese. Eggplant, red kuri squash, and lamb, for example, are scrumptious in this crumble with nutty accents. It's also a dish that gets better the second day.

Note: you can replace red kuri squash with another winter squash.

Serves 4

For the crumble topping:
⅓ cup (40 g; 1 ½ oz) millet flour
¼ cup (45 g; 1 ½ oz) brown rice flour
½ teaspoon ground cumin
⅓ cup (40 g; 1 ½ oz) pine nuts
1 ½ oz (40 g) walnuts, coarsely chopped
1 tablespoon chopped flat-leaf parsley

¼ cup (30 g; 1 oz) grated Emmentaler cheese
Sea salt and pepper
6 tablespoons (85 g; 3 oz) unsalted butter, at room temperature, diced

For the vegetables and meat:
3 tablespoons olive oil and more for the mold
¼ red onion, chopped
1 celery branch, diced

1 teaspoon ground cumin
2 garlic cloves, minced
14 oz (400 g) ground lamb
4 tomatoes, blanched, peeled, cored, seeded, and diced
1 tablespoon sun-dried tomato paste
1 medium Italian eggplant, diced
1 cup (125 g; 4 ½ oz) red kuri squash, peeled and diced
5 sage leaves, chopped
Sea salt and pepper

To make the topping: In a bowl, combine the flours, cumin, pine nuts, walnuts, parsley, and cheese. Season with salt and pepper. Add the butter and work with your fingers until crumbles form. Cover and refrigerate while you prepare the vegetables and meat.

To make the vegatables and meat: In a large sauté pan, heat 2 tablespoons of the oil over medium heat. Add the onion, celery, and cumin. Cook, stirring occasionally, without browning, until soft, about 4 minutes. Add the garlic and continue to cook for 2 minutes. Add the meat and cook through about 5 minutes. Add the tomato and tomato paste and cook for 3 more minutes. Add the eggplant and cook for 5 minutes. Add the squash and sage, and season with salt and pepper. Simmer for 30 minutes, uncovered, stirring occasionally.

In the meantime, preheat the oven to 400°F (200°C). Brush a 10-inch mold with oil and set aside. Transfer the vegetables and meat into the dish and spoon the crumble on top. Place the crumble in the oven and bake for 25 to 30 minutes, until golden on top. Serve immediately.

CASUAL DINNERS
WITH FRIENDS

We met our Dutch friends Mary and Frank the year I moved
to Boston. Philip and I were living in a cute red brick–walled
apartment in Brighton; we lived on the third floor and they
were on the first. We became best friends over many things:
walking on the beach, riding our bikes by the river, hiking in
the White Mountains, watching foreign movies, traveling, Danish furniture—and food. They were the family we didn't have
close by; they were the ones we called late in the afternoon to
ask whether they had dinner plans—and they were enthusiastic
cooks too!

Most of the time, we'd gather our efforts and cook together,
ending up either *chez nous* (at our place) upstairs, or *chez eux* (at
their place) downstairs. It would often start like this: We would
speak on the phone, make a rough plan, and scan quickly
through our fridges to improvise what we were going to cook
with the ingredients at hand. Most of the time, it was honest,
humble food; satisfying enough that after dinner, we'd eventually fall asleep on the floor—Frank and Philip mastered that
skill especially well, like true professionals of the art.

I liked to cook risottos and pasta with fresh seasonal vegetables, and I always had inspiration to bake savory tarts. Frank,

on the other hand, enjoyed baking bread and preparing stews and Indonesian dishes. "Indonesian food is quite common in the Netherlands," he explained when I asked, intrigued. "The spices, yum yum . . . so I like to cook it at home too," he went on. Naturally, seeing him cook dishes I knew so little about increased my curiosity to experiment with them. We often finished our meal with a simple dessert—yogurt, a fresh fruit salad, a homemade cake, or anything involving chocolate.

When they eventually returned to the Netherlands we were sad to see them go, but we've kept the memory of our meals together. Somehow, they taught me to see what I like in a casual dinner with friends—the fact that it's spontaneous and it feels comfortable and homey; it's dinner even if the house is messy and there's paperwork around or laundry to do. It's the moment in the day when we can relax and casually have a good time around homemade foods. And it always feels heartwarming, like home.

Salmon and watercress quiche

Serves 4

You will need: a 10-inch quiche mold

Sweet rice, quinoa, and amaranth
   crust (see Basic Recipes, page
   23)

7 oz (200 g) watercress or baby
   spinach

4 tablespoons olive oil

1 cup (235 ml) whole milk

1 bay leaf

Sea salt and pepper

1 pound 2 oz (500 g) skinned salmon

4 large eggs

¾ cup (175 ml) heavy cream

Dash of freshly grated nutmeg

1 tablespoon chopped dill

A few sage leaves, chopped

2 small leeks, white part only, finely
   chopped

1 shallot, finely chopped

1 egg white, lightly beaten with
   a fork

I come from the Lorraine region of France where we make and eat the traditional *quiche lorraine*—a deep savory tart baked with an egg batter, lard, and *crème fraîche* filling. However, this dish has never been my favorite. Instead, I like my quiches cooked with vegetables or fish, like in this recipe. The bitter, peppery taste of watercress combined with rich salmon poached in milk makes for an exact balance of flavors on your plate. This quiche is simply exquisite—and can always be made ahead of time!

Preheat the oven to 400°F (200°C) and butter a 10-inch quiche mold (quiche molds have higher sides than regular tart molds).

To prepare the watercress, start by cutting off the leaves and discarding the longer stems. Make sure to wash it a few times until the water is clear to completely remove the dirt. Dry the cleaned watercress in a salad spinner.

In a sauté pan, heat 2 tablespoons of the oil over medium heat. Add the watercress and sauté for about 3 minutes, stirring, until soft. Transfer to a colander and squeeze out the excess water between your fingers. Set the pan aside to use later. Finely chop the watercress and set aside.

In a pot, heat ¾ cup of the milk with the bay leaf and a pinch of sea salt and pepper. When just beginning to simmer, add the salmon and poach it for 3 minutes. Remove from the heat, cover, and let infuse for 10 minutes. Remove the salmon and crumble it into a bowl, making sure to discard the bones; set aside.

In a bowl, beat the eggs with the cream and the remaining ¼ cup milk. Season with sea salt and pepper and add the nutmeg, dill, and sage; set aside.

In the same sauté pan you used for the watercress, heat the remaining 2 tablespoons oil over medium heat. Add the leeks and shallot and cook for about 5 minutes without browning, stirring, until soft. Remove from the heat and stir in the watercress; set aside.

Roll and cut the dough to fit inside the mold. Arrange the dough inside the mold and using a fork, make small holes at the bottom.

Prebake for 10 minutes (see Basic Cooking Techniques, page 27, for instructions). Remove the parchment paper and weights and brush the crust with the egg white. Return to the oven and bake for 5 more minutes. Add the vegetables and crumbled salmon to the crust and pour the egg batter over the top.

Bake the quiche for 30 to 35 minutes (20 minutes if you're making individual quiches), or until the top is golden and the egg flan is set. Let rest for 10 minutes before cutting; serve with a green salad.

My simplified fish bouillabaisse
with saffron-flavored rouille

Pronounce the word *bouillabaisse* and you might hear, "It's too long to make and I cannot find the right fish." Fair enough—an authentic *bouillabaisse* requires time. Purists will even add that it needs *rascasse*, a fish commonly found in the South of France where *bouillabaisse* originates. But the truth is that you can make a bouillabaisse any way you like. I prefer to enjoy a variant that follows my imagination and that invariably prompts us to lick our fingers clean after we eat. With its firm meaty texture, monkfish is particularly excellent in this slow-cooked fish stew, and is delicious paired with the earthy aroma of saffron and the aniselike taste of fennel.

Of course, don't forget to serve the *bouillabaisse* with *rouille*, the typical sauce that accompanies the dish, and with toasted slices of baguette and grated cheese. If you close your eyes, you might almost feel like you are in Marseilles.

Serves 4

For the saffron and paprika *rouille*:
1 whole garlic clove, peeled
Sea salt
Pinch of saffron
Pinch of paprika
1 extra-fresh large egg yolk, cold
¼ to ⅓ cup (60 to 80 ml) olive oil

For the *bouillabaisse*:
4 cups (945 ml) fish stock or chicken stock
¼ teaspoon saffron threads

1 tablespoon (14 g; ½ oz) unsalted butter
1 tablespoon olive oil
1 yellow onion, finely chopped
3 garlic cloves, minced
2 twigs of fresh thyme
1 celery stalk, diced
2 large tomatoes, blanched, peeled, seeded, and diced
1 tablespoon double-concentrated tomato paste
12 small fingerling potatoes, cut into 1-inch pieces
1 fennel bulb, sliced
1 bay leaf

½ cup (120 ml) dry white wine or white vermouth
Sea salt and pepper
1 pound (450 g) Alaskan salmon, skinned and cut into 2-inch pieces
1 pound (450 g) monkfish, cut into 2-inch pieces
8 large scallops
12 large shrimp, peeled and deveined but with tails on
Fresh flat-leaf parsley, to serve
Toasted slices of baguette
Freshly grated Parmesan cheese, to serve

Preheat the oven to 400°F (200°C).

To prepare the *rouille*: In a small mortar, crush the garlic with a pinch of sea salt. Add the saffron, paprika, and egg yolk and mix well. Let rest for 5 minutes, then add the oil slowly, while whisking. The sauce thickens as you whisk in the oil. Add enough oil to reach the texture you like. Cover with plastic wrap and refrigerate until ready to use.

To prepare the *bouillabaisse*: In a small pot, heat the stock and keep warm.

In a bowl, combine the saffron with a little of the warm broth and let infuse for 10 minutes.

In a heavy ovenproof casserole, melt the butter over medium heat and add the oil. Add the onion and cook for 2 to 3 minutes, stirring, until soft. Add the garlic and thyme and cook for 1 more minute, then add the celery. Continue to cook for 2 to 3 minutes, stirring occasionally, until the celery softens. Add the tomatoes and tomato paste and cook for 4 minutes, stirring occasionally, until the vegetables soften. Add the potatoes and fennel and cook for 4 more minutes. Then add the bay leaf, wine, saffron, and broth. Season with sea salt and pepper, then cover and bring to a simmer.

Transfer the pot to the oven and cook for 20 minutes. Add the salmon and monkfish and return to the oven for 15 more minutes. Add the scallops and shrimp and return to the oven for 5 more minutes. Discard the bay leaf and thyme.

To serve, ladle the bouillabaisse in deep plates and sprinkle with parsley. Spread *rouille* on the toasted slices of baguette and add to the plates. Serve with grated cheese.

Lemon and honey-flavored chicken

with zebra tomatoes and haricots verts

The lemon juice, honey, and oregano in which this chicken dish is cooked give you a scrumptious zesty sauce to dip your bread in! Sometimes I like to add grated ginger to give the dish an exotic hint—also because anything cooked with ginger makes me happy. For more flavor, marinate the meat for an hour before cooking it, or even brine it first, but if you're short on time, skipping these steps is just fine. Zebra tomatoes have a subtly sweet taste that I find irresistible. If you have difficulty finding them, use another variety instead. And as for the oregano, any Mediterranean herbs, such as thyme or marjoram, for example, work well too.

Serves 4

Juice of 1 lemon

2 tablespoons honey

1 tablespoon chopped fresh
oregano

3 garlic cloves, minced

¼ cup (60 ml) olive oil

Sea salt and pepper

4 chicken legs (about 2 pounds;
900 g), each cut in half, or
8 drumsticks

4 green zebra tomatoes,
quartered

½ cup unpitted black kalamata olives

¼ cup cold water

1 pound (450 g) *haricots verts* (thin
French green beans)

1 tablespoon chopped flat-leaf
parsley

In a bowl, combine the lemon juice, honey, oregano, garlic, and oil. Season with sea salt and pepper and mix until smooth. Arrange the chicken legs in an oven dish and coat them with this sauce. Cover with plastic wrap and refrigerate for 30 minutes.

Preheat the oven to 375°F (190°C). Add the tomatoes, olives, and ¼ cup water to the chicken, place in the oven, and bake for 50 minutes, or until golden brown.

While the chicken is cooking, blanch the *haricots verts* in a pot of salted boiling water for 5 minutes. Drain and rinse them under cold water to stop them from cooking; set aside. Five minutes before the chicken is done, add the *haricots verts* to the dish. When you're ready to serve, add the parsley. Enjoy with steamed potatoes, mashed potatoes, or steamed rice on the side—and don't forget the bread to sop up the sauce.

Note on brining meat: When you take the time to brine legs of chicken, for example, you end up with extremely tender meat. The way I do it is as follows: For the brine, count about 1 quart (4 cups) water for every pound (450 g) of chicken. For 2 quarts, use ½ cup kosher salt, 3 tablespoons of sea salt, and 4 tablespoons of fine sugar. Combine the ingredients in a large bowl and immerse the chicken legs in this salty water. Cover and refrigerate for a minimum of 2 hours. When ready to use, drain the chicken and pat it dry with paper towels.

Summer vegetable tian

Oh the joy of a melt-in-the-mouth vegetable *tian*! I have a true weakness for this dish. Originally from the South of France, a *tian* is a dish in which summer vegetables—similar to those used in a *ratatouille*—are layered and baked slowly in a low-heated oven. The result is melting layers of flavors and scents that transport you to the Mediterranean. During the summer, when I can get wonderfully aromatic vegetables at the farmers' market, this is a meal we enjoy weekly. Also, to simplify dinner when you're busy, prepare the dish ahead of time, or even the day before.

Serves 4

1 tablespoon chopped lemon thyme
    or regular thyme
¼ cup chopped basil
5 garlic cloves, minced
2 Italian eggplants (280 g; 10 oz),
    sliced into thin rounds
Sea salt
Olive oil
2 zucchini (400 g; 14 oz), thinly
    sliced (use a mandoline if you
    have one)
3 to 4 ripe tomatoes (550 g;
    19 ½ oz), thinly sliced
2 fennel bulbs (280 g; 10 oz), thinly
    sliced (use a mandoline
    if you have one)
Pepper

In a small bowl, combine the chopped herbs and garlic.

Place the eggplant slices in a colander and sprinkle them with sea salt. Let them rest for 30 minutes so the moisture releases. Pat dry with paper towels.

Preheat the oven to 320°F (160°C).

Brush a large oven dish with oil and layer your vegetables into it in this order: 1 layer of tomatoes, 2 layers of zucchini, 1 of eggplant, 1 of fennel; repeat this pattern until you run out of vegetables, adding some of the chopped herbs and garlic each time between layers. Season with sea salt and pepper and drizzle generously with oil.

Place the *tian* in the oven and cook for 1 hour and 15 minutes to 1 hour and 30 minutes, until the vegetables are tender when pierced with a fork. Check regularly to make sure that they do not brown too quickly, covering the dish with a piece of foil paper if that's the case. Serve warm with a green salad and grilled meat or fish.

Spaghetti with fresh corn, crab, peas, and cherry tomatoes

It's only when I moved to the United States that I discovered the true taste of corn—and how delicious it is. I had actually never eaten fresh corn before, as in France, it's uncommon and fairly difficult to find. This quick pasta dish makes an appetizing dinner to enjoy with friends. Corn reveals sweet flavors that pair remarkably well with fresh crab and the citruslike aroma of marjoram. If you cannot find marjoram, use another Mediterranean herb, such as oregano or thyme.

Serves 4

For the tomatoes:

2 cups (350 g; 12 ½ oz) cherry
    tomatoes
2 garlic cloves, minced
1 teaspoon light Muscovado sugar
1 teaspoon chopped marjoram
3 tablespoons olive oil
Sea salt and pepper

2 ears of corn, shucked (about
    1 cup corn kernels)
1 cup (130 g: 4 ½ oz) shelled green
    peas (fresh or frozen)
12 oz (340 g) spaghetti
2 tablespoons olive oil
1 small red onion or shallot, finely
    chopped
2 garlic cloves, minced
2 oz (60 g) chopped *coppa* or
    pancetta
⅓ cup (80 ml) dry white wine
1 tablespoon chopped
    marjoram
6 oz (175 g) cooked fresh
    crabmeat
¾ cup (175 ml) chicken broth
Sea salt and pepper
½ cup (120 ml) heavy cream
1 tablespoon chopped flat-leaf
    parsley

To prepare the tomatoes: Preheat the oven to 350°F (180°C).

In a bowl, gently toss the tomatoes with the garlic, sugar, marjoram, and oil, and season with sea salt and pepper. Transfer to an oven dish and bake for 25 minutes; when done, turn off the heat and keep warm in the oven.

In the meantime, blanch the corn in a large pot of boiling salted water. Remove from the water and let cool. Add the peas to the boiling water and cook for 2 minutes; drain and rinse under cold water to stop the cooking; set aside. Using a sharp knife, cut the kernels off the corn; set aside.

Cook the spaghetti according to the instructions on the package. Drain and return to the pot. Gently toss the pasta with 1 tablespoon of the oil; cover to keep warm and set aside.

In a sauté pan, heat the remaining tablespoon oil over medium heat. Add the onion, garlic, and *coppa,* and cook, without browning, for 3 minutes, stirring occasionally. Add the white wine and bring to a simmer. Increase the heat to medium-high and let the wine reduce for 2 minutes. Add the marjoram, crab, and chicken stock. Season with sea salt and pepper and let simmer, uncovered, for 5 minutes. Add the heavy cream, corn, and peas, and simmer for 3 more minutes. Stir in the parsley. Add the sauce to the spaghetti and toss, and top with the baked tomatoes to serve.

Hachis parmentier

with chicken, lime, and coriander

Every time my mother cooks a *pot-au-feu*, she uses the beef leftovers to make a *hachis parmentier*, a dish made with a layer of ground meat, one of mashed potatoes, and one of grated cheese (the French equivalent to a shepherd's pie). It was—and still *is*—one of my favorite homey foods on a wintry day, and the best way to use any leftovers of a meat stew. Here, I use chicken to give the dish an unique flair and serve the dish in individual glasses. The rich layers of food stand out through the glass and are sure to impress your guests.

Serves 4

You will need: a 9-by-12-inch baking dish, or 4 individual oven-safe glasses

For the chicken:
2 tablespoons olive oil
1 teaspoon ground coriander
1 medium red onion, coarsely
    chopped
Dash of chile flakes
Finely grated zest and juice of
    1 organic lime

14 oz (400 g) chicken breast, or left-
    overs of cooked chicken meat,
    coarsely chopped
Sea salt and pepper
⅓ cup (80 ml) unsweetened coco-
    nut milk
1 tablespoon chopped cilantro
Butter, for the baking dish

For the vegetables:
1 pound 13 ounces (800 g) baking
    potatoes, peeled and diced
7 oz (200 g) carrots, peeled and
    coarsely chopped

Sea salt and pepper
½ cup plus 3 tablespoons
    (150 ml) whole milk
⅓ cup (80 ml) unsweetened coco-
    nut milk
Dash of freshly grated nutmeg
3 tablespoons butter, diced
1 oz finely grated Parmesan cheese

To prepare the chicken: In a frying pan, heat the oil over medium heat. Add the coriander and cook for about 1 minute, until fragrant. Add the onion, chile flakes, and lime zest and cook for 3 minutes, stirring. Add the chicken, season with sea salt and pepper, and cook for 2 more minutes. Add the coconut milk and simmer, covered, for 5 minutes.

Transfer the chicken and sauce to the bowl of a food processor and add the lime juice and cilantro. Purée to a medium to fine consistency; set aside.

Preheat the oven to 400°F (200°C) and butter an 9-by-12-inch baking dish; set aside.

To prepare the vegetables: In a pot, combine the potatoes and carrots. Add sea salt and cover with water. Bring to a boil, then reduce the heat, cover, and cook until the vegetables are fork-tender, about 20 minutes. Drain.

Using a food mill or ricer, purée the vegetables. Season with sea salt and pepper and stir in the milk, coconut milk, nutmeg, and 2 tablespoons of the butter.

Layer the chicken into the dish and top with the vegetables. Add the cheese and finish with the remaining 1 tablespoon butter, spread evenly across.

Place in the oven and bake for 20 minutes, or until the top is golden. Serve warm with a salad.

Arugula salad

with beets, radishes, shaved fennel, and feta cheese

This salad is exactly the kind of refreshing food that makes me excited and happy at the thought of starting a meal. Arugula is a longtime favorite green, and I like to vary the ingredients in the recipe—goat cheese instead of feta, pine nuts instead of hazelnuts, even adding pieces of fresh fruit—to enhance the peppery taste of the greens. This way the salad has both crunch and a welcoming personality.

Note: The thing that really transforms this salad from good to outstanding is slicing the radish and fennel as thinly as possible—I highly recommend using a mandoline if you have one. Also, you'll notice that I call for French feta cheese. I know, I know, the French are not known for feta, but I still prefer it, as it's less salty than its Greek parent.

To prepare the vinaigrette: In a small bowl, add the ingredients in this order: sea salt, pepper, mustard, coriander, vinegar, olive oil, and hazelnut oil. Whisk to emulsify. Stir in the chopped herbs; set aside.

To prepare the salad: Toast the hazelnuts in a frying pan over medium heat for about 4 to 5 minutes, or until lightly browned and fragrant. Place them in a clean kitchen towel and rub them to remove the skins. When they are cool enough to be handled, chop them coarsely; set aside.

In a large bowl, combine the arugula, beet, fennel, radishes, and feta cheese. Toss gently with the vinaigrette. Add the Parmesan cheese and toss gently again. Top with the toasted hazelnuts and serve.

Serves 4 to 6

For the vinaigrette:
Sea salt and pepper
½ teaspoon French Dijon mustard
½ teaspoon ground coriander
2 tablespoons white wine vinegar
4 tablespoons olive oil
2 tablespoons hazelnut oil
1 tablespoon chopped cilantro
1 tablespoon chopped dill

For the salad:
1 oz (30 g) hazelnuts
4 packed cups (100 g; 3 ½ oz) arugula
1 cooked beet, peeled and diced
1 fennel bulb, core removed and thinly sliced
5 to 6 pink radishes, thinly sliced
⅓ cup (50 g; 1 ¾ oz) crumbled French feta cheese
Finely grated Parmesan cheese, to taste

Vegetable tajine

Serves 4

2 tablespoons olive oil

1 small red onion, finely chopped

2 garlic cloves, minced

2 thyme twigs

½ teaspoon ground turmeric

½ teaspoon ground cumin

½ teaspoon ground coriander

½ teaspoon ground cinnamon

1 tomato, blanched, peeled, seeded,
   and diced

1 tablespoon double-concentrated
   tomato paste

4 carrots, peeled and sliced

12 oz (350 g) butternut squash,
   peeled, seeded and diced

1 fennel bulb, sliced

2 sweet potatoes, peeled and diced

1 bay leaf

Sea salt and pepper

1 cup (235 ml) homemade vegetable
   broth (see Basic Recipes, page
   25) or chicken broth

1 cup (150 g; 5 ¼ oz) cooked chickpeas

1 ½ cups (170 g; 6 oz) cauliflower
   florets

½ cup raisins, soaked in hot water for
   10 minutes

Chopped cilantro, to serve

There's something extremely satisfying about bringing an aromatic dish of tender vegetables to the table. It's about the spices that infuse in the house as the food cooks slowly in the oven. It's about the sauce in which the vegetables stew, in which you'll inevitably want to dip a piece of bread. This *tajine* has that magic. It's excellent served with quinoa, rice, or couscous to make a full dinner. You'll beg for left-overs.

Preheat the oven to 350°F (180°C).

In a large sauté pan or *tajine* dish, heat the oil over medium heat. Add the onion and cook for 3 minutes, without browning, stirring, until soft. Add the garlic, thyme, and spices and cook for 1 more minute, or until fragrant. Add the tomato and tomato paste and cook for 2 more minutes, or until the tomatoes soften. Add the carrots, butternut squash, fennel, and sweet potatoes and cook for about 7 minutes, stirring, until the vegetables start to soften. Add the bay leaf, season with sea salt and pepper, and add the stock and chickpeas. Bring to a simmer.

Cover, transfer to the oven, and cook for 40 minutes. Add the cauliflower and raisins and continue to cook for 20 more minutes. Discard the bay leaf and thyme and add the cilantro. Serve with a grain such as couscous, millet, polenta, or quinoa.

White lentil soup

with chorizo, poached eggs, and paprika cream

"Elle a vraiment du caractère, ta soupe!" ("Your soup has a ton of character!") my father exclaimed while eating quickly, as he always does. My parents were visiting us for two weeks — it was February in Boston. Winter. We could feel the wind and snow falling outside. And it was exactly the kind of rustic food that we felt like eating for dinner. Perfect with a loaf of crusty country bread on the side, and even some grated cheese if we felt like it.

Serves 6

2 tablespoons olive oil

2 thyme twigs

1 teaspoon ground cumin

½ teaspoon ground turmeric

1 large shallot, chopped

1 large leek, white part only, finely chopped

2 celery stalks, finely chopped

24 thin slices of spicy chorizo

2 large tomatoes, blanched, peeled, cored, seeded, and diced

1 tablespoon double-concentrated tomato paste

2 cups white lentils, rinsed and sorted

2 large carrots, peeled and diced

1 cup peeled and diced butternut squash or kabocha squash

4 cups chicken stock or homemade vegetable broth (see Basic Recipes, page 25)

4 cups (945 ml) cold water

¼ teaspoon saffron threads

2 bay leaves

3 cilantro stems with leaves, plus more leaves to serve

Sea salt and pepper

For the egg:

Pinch of sea salt

1 tablespoon white wine vinegar

6 extra-fresh large eggs

Crème fraîche, to serve

Ground paprika, to serve

In a large pot, heat the oil over medium heat. Add the thyme, cumin, turmeric, shallot, leek, and celery and cook, stirring, for 5 minutes, without browning, until fragrant and the vegetables start to soften. Add the slices of chorizo and cook for 2 minutes, stirring. Add the tomatoes and tomato paste and cook for 1 minute. Add the lentils, carrots, and squash and cook for 1 minute, then add the stock, water, saffron, bay leaves, and cilantro stems, and season with salt and pepper. Cover and simmer the soup for 25 minutes, or until all the vegetables and the lentils are fork-tender. Discard the thyme and bay leaves and keep warm on the stove while you prepare the eggs.

To prepare the egg: Bring a large pot of water to a boil. Add a generous pinch of sea salt and the vinegar. Bring to a simmer. Break 1 egg into a small cup and carefully transfer the egg into the simmering water. Cook for 2 to 3 minutes, until the egg white is set but the yolk is still runny. Remove with a slotted spoon and transfer to a paper towel. Repeat with the other eggs.

To serve, ladle the soup into deep bowls, sprinkle with the cilantro leaves, and add a heaping tablespoon of *crème fraîche* to each. Top each bowl with a poached egg and a dash of paprika.

To serve, ladle the soup into deep bowls, sprinkle with the cilantro leaves, and add a heaping tablespoon of *crème fraîche* to each. Top each bowl with a poached egg and a dash of paprika.

SOPHISTICATED AND ELEGANT DINNERS

Elegant dinners...you know the kind; those evenings that trigger the *wow* effect among your guests, with everything looking pretty and tasty, and everyone around the table feeling cheery and relaxed. These evenings feed my creativity to prepare beautiful out-of-the-ordinary foods—a good thing, since they feed us too.

To begin, these dinners are a good excuse for me to wear one of my favorite aprons (I *do* have a colorful collection hanging in the kitchen that cheers the wall, and me). I know well that my hair will be all tangled and my cheeks pink and flushed from the heat and activity in the kitchen. I love it! If our dinner happens on a Saturday, I will typically start my food preparations on Thursday or Friday. I imagine the menu for days, with ideas passing through my head day and night—incessantly. *Maybe this? Maybe that? Or what about this?* I'll admit that sometimes this constant brain activity drives me, and Philip, wild. But mostly it's fun. Open food magazines and cookbooks, and pieces of paper with cooking notes will lie everywhere around the house to inspire me, and for once, I won't mind the clutter. But when the evening finally arrives, the clutter is replaced by my favorite linens, freshly ironed, a colorful bouquet of ranunculus to brighten the table, and decanted bottles of wine patiently awaiting the guests—this is when I know that the evening will be delicious from start to finish. No matter the mess and heat and activity in the kitchen, it's worth it.

I held one of these special dinners during the summer I was pregnant with Lulu, not caring that I was seven months into my pregnancy and much slower than usual to move and work in the kitchen. It was a cool, comfortable evening, the kind that makes you wish summer would never end, and I wanted the evening to be delicious all the way through. So naturally, I planned a light and refreshing menu to suit the mood. We started with thin slices of prosciutto stuffed with fresh herbs, ricotta cheese, and sun-dried tomatoes that Philip paired with a terrific Alsatian white wine. Next we had *mille-feuilles* of shrimp, grapefruit, and avocado dressed in citrus vinaigrette, always a winning combination, followed by a creamy, silky dish of gorgonzola risotto. We ate and drank and chatted and laughed and ate more, and before we knew it, the clock struck midnight.

"Dessert anyone?" I asked. We couldn't skip it! It had taken me two days to make a strawberry and raspberry *charlotte*, the *crème de la crème* of summer desserts.

"Did you make the ladyfingers too?" my friend Helen asked while studiously licking the sweet raspberry cream spread on her lips. She was pregnant too, so her appetite was ferocious.

"Mais oui!"

The spongy biscuits carried just the right amount of sugar and they melted like snow in the mouth.

"That's a lot of work!" she said without looking up from her plate. I smiled—I could hear that the tone of her voice was whispering "thank you, thank you!"

She didn't know it, but watching her enjoy her food was the best way she could find to thank me—besides feeling fulfilled from creating these scrumptious pretty foods, seeing my friends happy was what I wanted. What could be sweeter than building wonderful memories with friendship and food at its center?

Dressed-up salmon ceviche

To this day, I find that a *ceviche* is the best way to enjoy fresh fish. This *ceviche* recipe makes a colorful appetizer with tons of zest and crunch as it reveals refreshing pieces of fruit and flavors of ginger, cumin, and lime. I've also prepared the recipe with cooked lobster meat before—after going lobster fishing!—with similarly excellent results. I recommend that you chop all the ingredients to the same size, a half inch being ideal, and use a ring mold to plate the *ceviche*. Also, prepare this appetizer as close to serving time as possible if using fresh salmon.

Serves 6

You will need: a 4-inch ring mold

Sea salt and pepper

¼ teaspoon ground cumin

Finely grated zest and juice of
   1 large organic lime

1½ teaspoons finely grated fresh
   ginger

1 tablespoon chopped cilantro

2 tablespoons olive oil, plus more to
   drizzle

1 pink grapefruit

7 oz (200 g) sushi-grade salmon or
   150 g (5 ¼ oz) drained cooked
   lobster meat

¼ English cucumber, peeled, seeded,
   and diced

1 pink lady apple, cored and diced,
   drizzled with lime juice

1 avocado, peeled, pitted, and diced,
   drizzled with lime juice

2 tablespoons plus 1 teaspoon finely
   chopped red onion

2 tablespoons pomegranate seeds,
   to top

Watercress or mâche leaves, to serve

Have 6 appetizer plates ready.

In a small bowl, combine a pinch of sea salt and pepper, the cumin, lime zest and juice, ginger, cilantro, and oil and whisk to emulsify.

With a sharp serrated knife, peel the skin and pith from the grapefruit. Cut the fruit into segments, discarding the membrane. Dice and set side. Dice the fish. In a large bowl, gently toss the salmon, cucumber, apple, grapefruit, avocado, and 2 tablespoons of the red onion. Drizzle with the dressing and toss again. Let cool in the fridge for 10 minutes.

Place the ring mold on top of 1 plate. Pack one-sixth of the *ceviche* into the mold and remove the ring. Repeat with the other 5 plates. Top with chopped red onion and pomegranate seeds. Drizzle with oil and decorate with watercress or mâche leaves. Serve immediately.

Drizzling lime on the fish "cooks" it, but without heat—the citric acid present in lime juice, and other citrus fruit, denatures the proteins in fish, as cooking would.

Pretty buckwheat, millet, and vegetable galettes

The first vacation I took with friends was when I was seventeen, and four of us drove to Brittany on the west coast of France. We were three girls and a boy, Pierre, the only one with a driving license; we felt free and bursting with life. One of the highlights of our trip was eating filled *galettes* (the French word for savory *crêpes* made with buckwheat flour) in the *crêperies* of Saint Malo and the small towns we drove through as we toured the area. I've been a lover of *galettes* ever since then.

Filled with finely grated, melt-in-the-mouth vegetables, these *galettes* are irresistible. They are baked in ramekins, which makes them look like pretty flowers once they are served on your plate. To save time, prepare the *galettes* a day ahead and reheat them for 15 minutes in an oven preheated to 300°F (150°C) when you are ready to serve.

Serves 4

You will need: four 6-oz ramekins and one 7-inch ring mold

For the buckwheat and millet galettes (makes four 8-inch galettes):
½ tablespoon safflower oil, plus more to oil the ramekins and cook the *galettes*
¼ cup (34 g; 1 oz) millet flour
2 tablespoons buckwheat flour
1 ½ tablespoons sweet rice flour
Pinch of sea salt
1 large egg
½ cup (120 ml) whole milk
¼ cup (60 ml) cold water

For the vegetables:
2 tablespoons olive oil
½ teaspoon ground cumin
1 small shallot, finely chopped
1 medium carrot, peeled and finely grated
1 medium parsnip, peeled and finely grated
1 small zucchini, finely grated
Sea salt and pepper
3 tablespoons mixed fresh herbs (chervil, cilantro, and dill)
1 large egg, lightly beaten with a fork
2 tablespoons *crème fraîche*
1 tablespoon whole milk

Oil the ramekins and set aside.

To prepare the *galettes*: In a bowl, sift the flours and add the sea salt. Make a hole in the middle and break the egg inside. Whisk while pouring in the milk slowly, until the batter is smooth. Add the water and oil and stir well. Cover the batter and let rest in the fridge for 2 hours. Bring back to room temperature and stir again.

In a *crêpe* pan, heat a little oil over medium heat. Pour enough batter to cover the bottom (about ¼ to ⅓ cup, depending on the size of your pan). Swirl quickly to coat the bottom of the pan, and cook for 1 to 2 minutes, until small bubbles form at the surface. Using a spatula, flip the *galette* and cook on the other side for 1 minute. Transfer the *galette* to a plate. Add oil in the pan between each *galette,* and repeat until you run out of batter.

Using a 7-inch ring mold, cut the *galettes* so that they are 7 inches in diameter and have clean edges. Place them in the ramekins and press them down lightly so that they pleat on the sides; set aside.

To prepare the vegetables: Preheat the oven to 350°F (180°C).

In a frying pan, heat the oil over medium heat. Add the cumin and shallot and cook for 2 minutes, stirring, without browning. Add the grated vegetables and season with sea salt and pepper. Cook for 4 minutes, stirring, until the vegetables are soft. Transfer to a bowl and let cool. Stir in the herbs, egg, *crème fraîche,* and milk.

Divide the vegetable mixture among the *galettes,* place in the oven, and bake for 25 to 30 minutes, until the egg flan is set. Serve as an appetizer with a side salad.

Multicolored beet, ricotta, and goat cheese mille-feuille

with hazelnut vinaigrette

Serves 4

You will need: a 2 ¾-inch-wide by 2 ¼-inch-tall ring mold

For the vinaigrette:

Sea salt and pepper, to taste

2 tablespoons sherry vinegar

6 tablespoons hazelnut oil

1 tablespoon chopped chives

1 shallot, finely chopped

For the *mille-feuilles*:

1 ½ oz (40 g) hazelnuts

1 cup (200 g; 7 oz) whole milk ricotta
    cheese

½ cup (100 g; 3 ½ oz) soft fresh goat
    cheese

1 scallion, white part only, finely
    chopped

2 tablespoons chopped chives

2 teaspoons sherry vinegar

2 teaspoons hazelnut oil

Sea salt and pepper

4 small cooked yellow beets, peeled

4 small cooked red beets, peeled

Handful of mâche salad or mixed
    greens, to serve

Some time ago I shared this recipe with my mother-in-law; she tells me it's one of her favorites to make when she has guests over for dinner. "It's so pretty! Everyone raves about it," she says delighted—instantly, that makes me blush! She also tells me that it makes a wonderful summer lunch plate by adding a few extra salad greens to the presentation. On top of its pretty looks, the combination of sherry vinegar and hazelnut oil makes the flavors of this dish remarkable.

To prepare the vinaigrette: In a bowl, add the ingredients in this order: sea salt, pepper, vinegar, and oil. Whisk to emulsify. Stir in the chives and shallot; set aside.

To prepare the *mille-feuilles*: Toast the hazelnuts in a frying pan over medium heat for about 4 to 5 minutes, or until lightly browned and fragrant. Place them in a clean kitchen towel and rub them to remove the skins. When they are cool enough to be handled, chop them coarsely; set aside.

Place the ricotta in a colander and let stand for 30 minutes to drain the excess water.

In a bowl, smooth the ricotta with a fork and combine with the goat cheese. Mix in the scallion, chives, vinegar, and oil and season with sea salt and pepper.

Cut 4 horizontal slices in each beet. Using a ring mold, cut each slice of beet with it. Place a slice of beet inside the ring mold and spread with a layer of ricotta. Add another slice of beet, using a different color this time, and spread with another layer of ricotta. Repeat until you have 4 beets layered with ricotta between each. Secure your *mille-feuille* with a few toothpicks and remove the ring mold carefully. Repeat to make the other 3 *mille-feuilles*. Once you are done, refrigerate the *mille-feuilles* for 1 hour minimum.

When you are ready to serve, use a very sharp knife to trim the *mille-feuilles* so they have clean edges. Transfer the *mille-feuilles* onto 4 serving plates and remove the toothpicks. Drizzle with the vinaigrette and serve with mâche salad and chopped hazelnuts.

There are two ways to cook the beets. Place them in a pot and cover with water. Bring to a boil and cook until it's easy to insert a knife in the middle. Or, wrap them in foil and bake them in the oven at 375°F (190°C), until it's easy to insert a knife in the middle. Depending on the size of the beets, the cooking time for both methods can vary from 45 minutes to over an hour. Check regularly to make sure the beets are well cooked. When they are cool enough to handle, you can peel them.

You will end up with leftover beets that, well, you can use for something else, or you can nibble on while preparing the food — never a bad thing to keep you company while cooking.

If you cannot find yellow beets, use red instead. The dish is scrumptious either way.

Corn timbale
with vanilla-flavored vinaigrette

Oh, the delicate aroma of vanilla seeds in a balsamic vinaigrette! Perhaps you'll find this combination surprising, but it's really what turns this summer appetizer into a memorable experience, as the sweet perfume of the spice harmoniously enhances the fresh corn. Dress the dish up in the shape of an eye-catching timbale: It's sure to please the crowd gathered at your table.

Toast the pine nuts in a frying pan for 2 minutes over medium heat, until fragrant and lightly colored; set aside to cool.

Butter four 8-oz ramekins and line with parchment paper; set aside.

Place the tomatoes in a colander and season with sea salt. Let rest for 30 minutes to drain excess water.

Boil the corn in salted water for 4 minutes. Rinse under cold water, and once cool enough to handle, use a sharp knife to cut the kernels off.

To prepare the vinaigrette: In a small bowl, combine a pinch of sea salt and pepper, the vanilla seeds, vinegar, and oil. Whisk to emulsify.

In a large bowl, gently toss the tomatoes, corn, shallot, cilantro, and gomasio. Stir in half of the dressing. Divide the salad among the ramekins. Cover with a small piece of parchment paper and place a weight on top (another cup, for example). Refrigerate like this for a minimum of 1 hour—more is even better.

To serve, have 4 appetizer plates handy. Remove the weights and top piece of parchment paper. One at a time, put a plate on top of the ramekin and flip it at the center of the plate. Remove the second piece of parchment paper carefully; repeat for the other 3 timbales. Drizzle the timbales with the remaining vinaigrette, and decorate each with cilantro leaves and the pine nuts.

Serves 4 as an appetizer

You will need: four 8-oz ramekins

Unsalted butter for ramekins

2 tablespoons pine nuts

2 to 3 vine tomatoes or heirloom tomatoes (about 1 pound; 450 g), blanched, peeled, seeded, and diced

Sea salt

2 ears of corn, shucked

1 shallot, finely chopped

2 tablespoons chopped cilantro, plus extra to serve

1 tablespoon gomasio or toasted sesame seeds

For the vinaigrette:

Sea salt and pepper

½ vanilla bean, split open and seeds scraped out

1 ½ tablespoons balsamic vinegar

3 tablespoons olive oil

Fish fillets
with vegetable ribbons en papillote

Bringing a *papillote* right from the oven to the table is like bringing a gift to each of your guests. "What is hiding inside it?" they'll wonder. It's truly delightful to watch them open the *papillotes* and see that they reveal aromatic flavors of steaming fish, cooking in its own juice, with pretty ribbons of colorful vegetables. Though I call for trout in this recipe, any fish fillet will work—choose your favorite. I've used snapper, salmon, char, and cod before, each time with delicious results

Serves 4

1 zucchini, sliced lengthwise (use a vegetable peeler or a mandoline if you have one)

1 carrot, peeled and sliced lengthwise (use a vegetable peeler or a mandoline if you have one)

1 leek, top and bottom parts trimmed off, thinly sliced lengthwise

1 small fennel bulb, thinly sliced (use a mandoline if you have one)

¼ red onion, thinly sliced

1-inch piece fresh ginger, peeled and finely grated

2 garlic cloves, minced

1 tablespoon chopped cilantro

1 tablespoon chopped flat-leaf parsley

Sea salt and pepper

2 Meyer lemons or regular lemons

4 red trout fillets with the skin (about 6 oz /170 g each)

Olive oil, to brush and drizzle

Preheat the oven to 420°F (215°C). Have cooking string and four 14-inch pieces of parchment paper handy.

In a large bowl, gently toss the zucchini, carrot, leek, fennel, onion, ginger, garlic, cilantro, and parsley and season with sea salt and pepper; set aside.

Grate the zest of 1 lemon and juice it. Slice the other lemon into thin rounds.

Using paper towels, pat the fish dry and season with sea salt and pepper.

Place one piece of parchment paper on a working surface in front of you. Brush the center with oil. Make a bed of vegetables in the middle and add the fish fillet with the skin facing up. Sprinkle with some lemon zest and drizzle with lemon juice. Finish with another layer of vegetables and drizzle with olive oil. Top with 2 slices of lemon. Lift the edges of the paper to meet at the top and fold down a few times to create a package; secure the ends with string. There should be enough space between the ingredients and edge of the paper for the pouches to puff.

Set on a rimmed baking sheet, and repeat to create the other 3 *papillotes*. Place in the oven and bake them for 15 minutes, or until the fish is firm to the touch—the thinner the vegetables and fish, the quicker the cooking time. Serve the *papillotes* as is, on a plate.

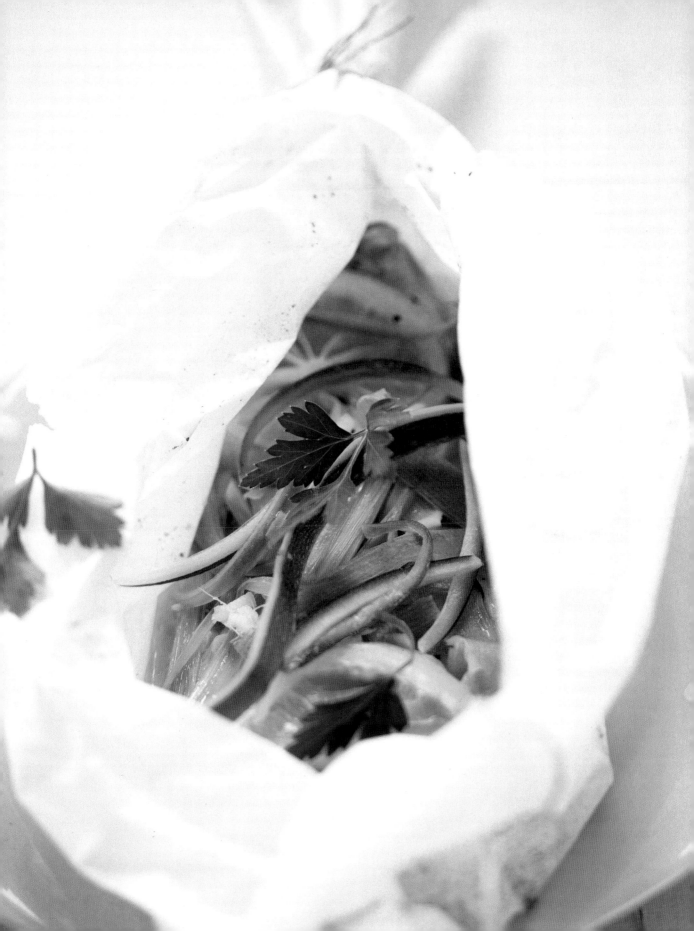

Arugula risotto
with basil and lemon

At times, when I think about a risotto, I feel I must have been Italian in a previous life. Cooking this wonderful dish is inspiring—and much easier than most people think. Each time I make it, I find it fascinating to see how the dish evolves from dry rice into a creamy rich concoction, which is exquisite no matter what flavors and ingredients you end up using. I cooked this particular risotto for the first time to surprise my parents on their wedding anniversary. I had picked fresh herbs in my brother's fantastic vegetable garden—incomparable—and absolutely adored the aromas and simplicity of this elegant dish. Eating it is like having the scents of summer concentrated onto your plate. To dress the dish up even more, sauté a few shrimp and serve them on top of the risotto.

Serves 4

Sea salt

3 packed cups (60 g; 2 oz) arugula

1 packed cup (25 g; 1 oz) basil leaves

1 packed cup (25 g; 1 oz) parsley leaves, plus a few sprigs to decorate

4 ½ cups (1 liter 60 ml) homemade vegetable broth (see Basic Recipes, page 25), or more as needed

2 tablespoons olive oil, plus more to drizzle

1 tablespoon (14 g; ½ oz) unsalted butter

1 shallot, coarsely chopped

1 leek, white part only, finely chopped

Finely grated zest of 1 organic lemon

1 ½ cups (300 g; 10 ½ oz) carnaroli rice, or another risotto rice, like Arborio or Vialone Nano

⅓ cup (80 ml) white vermouth or dry white wine

3 tablespoons mascarpone cheese

1 ½ oz (40 g) grated pecorino or Parmesan cheese, plus more to serve

Pepper

In a pot, combine a large volume of water with a generous pinch of sea salt and bring to boil. Add the arugula and herbs and blanch them for 30 seconds to 1 minute. Rinse under cold water and let cool. Squeeze the excess water out of the herbs by pressing with the tips of your fingers and finely chop; set aside.

In the same pot, warm the vegetable stock; set aside.

In a heavy pot, heat the oil and butter over medium heat. Add the shallot, leek, and lemon zest and cook, stirring, for 3 to 4 minutes, without browning, until soft and fragrant. Add the rice and cook for 1 minute, stirring constantly. Add the vermouth and cook, stirring, until the liquid is absorbed. Add 1 cup of broth and cook, stirring occasionally, until the rice has absorbed all the liquid. Add more broth and repeat. Watch that the heat is not too high so that the rice does not cook too quickly. Add the rest of the broth and the herbs, and continue to cook, stirring, until the herbs are well combined. Remove from the heat and stir in the mascarpone and the grated pecorino cheese. Season with pepper, cover, and set aside for 2 minutes.

Serve the risotto in shallow individual plates with a drizzle of oil and more grated pecorino cheese. Decorate with a few sprigs of parsley.

If you want to do some preparation ahead of time, you can freeze the cooked herbs. Once you have squeezed out the excess water, pack them tightly into an ice cube tray (makes 5 regular-size ice cubes). Add a little water and place in the freezer. There is no need to thaw the cubes before using them.

Salmon with an exotic spiced carrot sauce

This dish is wonderfully light and offers the accents I love in my food: zest and fresh healthy ingredients with cheerful bright colors. Choose extra-fresh salmon, as the fish should only be cooked *rosé* (rare) to keep its delicate flavor.

Serves 4

16 to 18 green asparagus spears

2 tablespoons olive oil

1½ pounds (675 g) salmon, skinned and cut into 1½-inch cubes

1 tablespoon chopped cilantro, to serve

Fleur de sel, to serve

For the sauce:

1½ cups (350 ml) freshly pressed carrot juice

1-inch piece fresh ginger, peeled and sliced

1 lemongrass stalk, outer leaves removed and thinly sliced

Finely grated zest and juice of 1 organic orange

1 garlic clove, sliced

Juice of 1 lime

1 teaspoon light Muscovado sugar

½ cup (120 ml) unsweetened coconut milk

Sea salt

Dash of cayenne pepper

Blanch the asparagus for 1 minute in a pot of boiling salted water. Drain and rinse under cold water to stop it from cooking, and when cool enough to handle, slice diagonally into 3 pieces each; set aside.

To prepare the sauce: In a pot, combine the carrot juice with the ginger, lemongrass, orange zest, and garlic. Bring to a simmer, and cook for 3 minutes. Remove from the heat, cover, and let infuse for 20 minutes. Add the orange juice, lime juice, and sugar and heat again until the sugar dissolves and the sauce is simmering. Strain and discard the spices. Stir in the coconut milk. Season with sea salt and add the cayenne pepper; cover and keep warm over low heat.

In a frying pan, heat the oil over medium heat. Add the cubes of salmon and cook on each side for 30 seconds so that the inside stays rare; remove from the heat and set aside.

Divide the fish among 4 plates and sprinkle with *fleur de sel.* Top with cilantro. Pour the sauce around the fish and serve with the asparagus along with steamed jasmine rice.

Mesclun salad

with cantaloupe, raspberries, and prosciutto

> In the summer, you'll love this bright herb salad with fruit accents as much as I do. Sometimes I'll eat a big bowl of it when I'm alone and need a treat, but it's also a perfect salad to start a dressed-up meal.

Serves 4

For the vinaigrette:

Pinch of sea salt

Pinch of cracked black or red
 peppercorns

2 tablespoons white balsamic
 vinegar or juice of 1 lime

1 whole garlic clove, peeled and
 crushed

1 teaspoon honey or apricot jam

5 tablespoons olive oil

1 tablespoon chopped dill

For the salad:

¼ cup (35 g; 1 ¼ oz) pine nuts

4 handfuls mesclun salad, washed
 and dried

12 small cherry tomatoes, cut in half

16 raspberries

8 small cantaloupe slices

4 slices of prosciutto or Jambon de
 Bayonne

Shaved pecorino cheese, to taste

To prepare the vinaigrette: In a bowl, combine the sea salt, pepper, vinegar, garlic, and jam. Add the oil and whisk to emulsify. Stir in the dill; set aside.

Toast the pine nuts in a frying pan over medium heat for 2 minutes, or until lightly browned and fragrant; set aside to cool.

Divide the salad greens among 4 plates. Add 3 cherry tomatoes, 4 raspberries, 2 slices of cantaloupe, and 1 slice of prosciutto to each plate. Drizzle the salad with the vinaigrette and top with shaved cheese and pine nuts.

Mille-feuille of shrimp, grapefruit, and avocado

This appetizer is simply gorgeous. It's one that offers a balancing show and makes the natural shapes of shrimp, avocado, and grapefruit stand out. So much so that, you might, just for a second, think it's too pretty to eat.

With a sharp serrated knife, peel the skin and pith from the grapefruit. Cut the fruit into segments, discarding the membrane and collecting the juice for the vinaigrette; set aside.

To prepare the vinaigrette: In a small bowl, add the ingredients in this order: sea salt and pepper, ginger, honey, grapefruit juice, and lime juice. Mix well and add the oil; whisk to emulsify. Set aside.

In a frying pan, heat the oil over medium heat. Add the shrimp and garlic and cook for about 2 minutes on each side, until the shrimp are pink. Sprinkle with the paprika and season with sea salt; set aside.

Cut the avocado in half and remove the pit. Using a mandoline or sharp knife, slice it lengthwise and drizzle with lime juice to prevent discoloration; set aside.

Take 4 small serving plates and assemble each plate as follows: In the middle of the plate, place a slice of avocado. Arrange 2 or 3 slices of grapefruit on top and then top with a shrimp. Add another slice of avocado and a few more grapefruit slices. Arrange the last shrimp on top. Sprinkle with gomasio and drizzle with a large tablespoon of vinaigrette. Serve immediately with chopped cilantro.

Serves 4 as an appetizer

For the salad:

2 small pink grapefruits

1 tablespoon olive oil

8 large shrimp, peeled and deveined, with tails intact

1 garlic clove, minced

Dash of paprika

Sea salt

1 avocado

Lime juice

1 teaspoon gomasio or toasted sesame seeds

Chopped cilantro, to serve

For the citrus vinaigrette:

Sea salt and pepper

1 inch piece fresh ginger, peeled and finely grated

1 teaspoon honey

2 tablespoons grapefruit juice (use the juice from cutting the fruit for the salad)

2 tablespoons lime juice

4 tablespoons olive oil

Gorgonzola and pear risotto
with rosemary and toasted walnuts

Serves 4

1 ½ oz (40 g) walnuts

3 red Anjou or Bartlett pears, peeled
    and cored

3 tablespoons (45 g; 1 ½ oz) unsalted
    butter, plus extra

4 ½ cups (1 liter 60 ml) chicken
    broth, or more as needed

1 tablespoon olive oil and more to
    serve

1 large shallot, finely chopped

1 leek, white part only, finely chopped

2 thyme sprigs

1 long rosemary sprig

1 ½ cups (300 g; 10 ½ oz) carnaroli
    rice, or another risotto rice, like
    Arborio or Vialone Nano

⅓ cup (80 ml) dry white vermouth
    (preferably Noilly Prat) or dry
    white wine

4 oz (120 g) Gorgonzola cheese,
    crumbled

3 tablespoons mascarpone cheese

1 ½ oz (40 g) grated Parmesan or
    pecorino cheese

Pepper

1 tablespoon chopped flat-leaf
    parsley

This scrumptious risotto really celebrates the flavors of fall; it's also Philip's absolute favorite dish. Every time I make it—never frequently enough in his opinion—he'll have lengthy conversations with me about how complex the flavors in the dish are, how creamy the rice is, and how he'd wished there would be more—his subtle (or not so subtle) way of asking, "Can you make it again soon?"

Toast the walnuts in a frying pan over medium heat for 4 to 5 minutes, or until lightly browned and fragrant. Let cool and coarsely chop; set aside.

Dice 2 of the pears and half of the third; thinly slice the remaining half.

In a frying pan, melt 1 tablespoon of the butter over medium heat. Add the diced pear and cook for 3 to 4 minutes, stirring, until the fruit softens; set aside. Add a little extra butter to the pan and cook the pear slices for 1 to 2 minutes on each side. Remove from the heat and set aside.

Heat the broth in a pot; keep warm.

In a heavy pot, melt the remaining 2 tablespoons butter over medium heat. Add the oil, then add the shallot, leek, rosemary, and thyme and cook for 2 to 3 minutes, stirring, until soft and fragrant. Add the rice and coat for 1 minute, stirring constantly. Add the vermouth and cook, stirring, until the liquid is absorbed. Add 1 cup of broth; cook, stirring occasionally. Wait until the rice has absorbed the liquid before adding more broth. Taste occasionally to see how done the risotto is; it should be creamy but still slightly al dente and the heat should be fairly low so that rice does not cook too quickly. When you only have ¾ cup of broth left and the risotto is almost done, stir in the diced pears and add the rest of the broth. Cook until the rice is done, stirring, and then remove from the heat. Stir in the Gorgonzola, mascarpone, and Parmesan cheeses and season with pepper; cover and set aside for 2 minutes. Discard the thyme and rosemary and stir in the parsley.

Divide the risotto among 4 plates and garnish with a slice of pear and the toasted walnuts. Drizzle with oil and serve.

Saffron-flavored crab and watercress soufflé

I had not thought about my mother's crab soufflé for a while, but images of the delicate puffed egg batter dipped into the lemon-flavored creamy sauce she served it with recently came floating back to my mind. It's a wonderful dish she only cooked for special occasions, Christmas being one. I asked for her recipe, but she regrettably told me she couldn't find it. So I improvised and created this recipe. Although it is not exactly like my mother's, this crab soufflé is utterly delicious. And it is bound to leave an impression on your guests, especially if you decide, as suggested, to make individual soufflés for each guest.

Serves 4 as an appetizer

You will need: four 10-ounce tall ramekins

4 packed cups (100 g; 3 ½ oz) watercress

1 cup (235 ml) whole milk

½ teaspoon saffron threads

2 tablespoons (30 g; 1 oz) unsalted butter, plus more for the ramekins

½ cup (60 g; 2 oz) finely grated Parmesan, plus more for the ramekins

2 tablespoons (20 g; ¾ oz) cornstarch

4 large eggs, separated, plus 1 egg white

6 oz (175 g) fresh crabmeat

Sea salt and pepper

1 tablespoon chopped flat-leaf parsley

Preheat the oven to 420°F (215°C).

To prepare the watercress, start by cutting off the leaves and discarding the longer stems. Make sure to wash it a few times until the water is clear to completely remove the dirt. Blanch it in a pot of water for 1 minute. Drain and rinse under cold water to stop it from cooking. When cool enough to be handled, press it between your fingers to squeeze out the excess water. Finely chop and set aside.

In a small pot, combine the milk with the saffron. Bring to a simmer, then remove from the heat; cover and leave to infuse for 15 minutes. The milk should remain warm to the touch when you dip a finger in it; gently reheat the milk if necessary.

Butter the ramekins and sprinkle each with grated cheese, covering the bottom and sides. Shake out the excess; set aside.

In a separate pot, melt the butter over medium-low heat. Stir in the cornstarch quickly and cook for 1 minute without browning, stirring. Increase the heat and pour the milk in gradually while stirring—the white sauce you're making is a *béchamel.* Cook it until it starts to bubble and becomes thicker. Remove from the heat, stir in the grated cheese, and let cool for 5 minutes. Stir in the egg yolks. Add the crab, watercress, and parsley and season with sea salt and pepper; set aside.

In a bowl, beat the egg whites with a pinch of sea salt until they form soft peaks. Gently fold into the crab batter.

Divide the batter among the molds, filling each ramekin three-quarters full. Place in the oven and bake for 25 to 30 minutes—the soufflés will rise and puff up and color nicely. Don't be tempted to open the oven before the cooking time is over, as the soufflé will deflate. Serve immediately, right out of the oven.

If you prefer to enjoy this recipe as a main course, use a 2-quart soufflé dish and change the recipe as follows: 1 ½ cups (350 ml) whole milk instead of 1 cup; 3 tablespoons butter instead of 2; 3 tablespoons cornstarch instead of 1; and 6 large eggs instead of 4. Proceed in exactly the same way when making the soufflé, but increase the cooking time to 45 minutes.

Desserts to Inspire

Everyday Baking 255

Beautiful and Irresistible Desserts 275

Quite often, people will tell you that differences are what keep a couple together. Philip excels at assembling things; I am useless at it. I like to do things quickly; he would rather take his time. I prefer the sheets of our bed to be neatly tucked; he'd happily sleep with his feet sticking out. But when it comes to dessert—whether it's a lemon tart, chocolate mousse, rhubarb crumble, *crème caramel, île flottante,* rice pudding, any of it—there is no difference between us at all. *Dessert . . .* it's an enchanting word.

Our mutual attraction to dessert is a blessing. I am able to play in my kitchen as much as I want, mixing, whipping, dipping my fingers in a bowl of chocolate, trying my hand at a new tart or muffins, and Philip—my best food critic—claps his hands, always excited and happy to taste what comes out of the oven, telling me honestly what he thinks. So we rarely finish a meal without a sweet touch. It's not necessarily fancy, mind you. On a regular day, we'd be satisfied with one or two pieces of dark chocolate, fruit, or a yogurt. Sometimes dessert would be raspberries and strawberries picked at the market. They'd be mashed or cut in small pieces and served with blond cane sugar, a drizzle of lime juice, coconut milk, and freshly chopped mint. The truth is, there's always something we can nibble on at home; naturally, since in our family, I am the baker.

Ideally, I start my day by baking a cake. A homey, comforting, and rustic *everyday* cake—one that is easily packed in my bag if I run out of the house for an errand, or nibbled on if we go hiking for the day. There are also the nights when I turn the kitchen into a mess just after cleaning it—have you noticed too how quickly this happens? It's easy to find reasons to justify this sudden urge. *"C'est thérapeutique."* ("It's therapeutic.") "It'll help me fall asleep." These are the things I tell Philip when he stares at me with a *what-the-hell-are-you-doing-it's-midnight* kind of look on his face. Inevitably, we laugh, feeling tired but greedy to taste whatever comes out of the oven, even if it's too hot and burns the tips of our tongues.

Desserts are to a meal what a dress is to a woman. They should fit for every occasion. During summer, light and fresh sweets with juicy berries are the desserts we turn to. In winter, we indulge in richer, more filling sweets—a loaf of almond dark chocolate cake baking in the oven while it snows outside and eaten while we cuddle on the couch with a book.

On the nights when we have friends over for dinner, I will naturally make something fancier—perhaps a raspberry *tiramisu* or a layered two-chocolate mousse cake—surely a dessert that prompts *ohhs* and *ahhs* when it is brought to the table. For Mother's Day, I will prepare a *charlotte aux fruits rouges,* my mother's absolute favorite. To make Philip happy, I'd make sure that there would always be a cherry *clafoutis* or a big bowl of warm rice pudding ready to be eaten somewhere in the house. I know that he wouldn't be able to resist—and me neither.

Dessert is all about love—a sweet taste that brings smiles to the faces of the people close to you. Even my father, who claims that he is not a *dessert-type-of-guy,* has his eyes lit with excitement when my mother brings her famous thin-crust plum tart to the table.

Dessert is one of the best parts of a meal: the most delicious way to seal the moment; what makes it memorable. After all, it's the last taste you keep in your mouth when a meal is over, so it'd better be something to win your heart.

222

FRENCH CHILDHOOD
MEMORIES

My mother introduced me to the world of baking. She taught me how to grow confident in the kitchen, holding the wooden spoon to work with sugar, butter, eggs, and flour. Most of her desserts were humble and earthy, which, I am sure, explains why if given the choice, I will always prefer a slice a rustic tart to a Parisian macaroon—it's undeniable that I learned by her side.

There were a few desserts that she made weekly. To start, there were her *petits pots de crème* that she flavored with chocolate or vanilla. My brother was always the one going after vanilla, while I preferred chocolate—that part hasn't changed a bit. Then, she educated me in the fantastic world of *île flottantes* (floating islands). Beside naming it *mon dessert préféré par dessus tout* (my favorite dessert above all), I was amused by the imagery it carried: I pictured that I was the white island floating forever in a bath of silky custard that I sipped slowly—I never wanted the moment to end. It was hard to imagine, but my brother liked this dessert even more than I did—and I was fast to learn this weakness of his. Whenever he and I argued, I used the dessert as a bribe to settle our argument, consequently learning how to make my first *île flottantes*. You should try this too, it works like magic.

My mother also taught me how to bake my first cake, a *mar-bré* (a marbled cake) flavored with chocolate and vanilla. Every Saturday, we'd bake two loaves because the first one always disappeared within a day. Then, when I was in seventh grade, *madeleines* entered my life thanks to Monsieur Hennequi's cooking class. How proud I felt to bring these buttery cakes home in my bag!

There were also my grandmother Louise's desserts. On weekends, when we visited her in the village next-door, she'd often have prepared a bowl of *riz au lait* (rice pudding). I liked to eat it sitting on my grandfather's lap, while we watched *Zorro* on TV in black and white. He and I had agreed that I couldn't leave before *Zorro* was over and my rice pudding plate was clean. Needless to say, our deal made me a very happy girl.

Making dessert came to me naturally because of all of these episodes in my younger years. And even if, over the years, I've moved on to more intricate baking projects, when I'm feeling nostalgic for my childhood—for France and my grandparents' house and *Zorro*—a rice pudding, an *île flottante*, or a *petit pot de crème* is what I bring to the table.

Petits pots de crème (little custards)

flavored with cardamom and vanilla

Makes six ⅔-cup jars

You will need six ⅔-cup glass jars

For the applesauce:

3 apples, peeled, cored, and diced
    (Cortland, Macoun, or McIntosh
    are good choices)

2 tablespoons blond cane sugar

1 tablespoon light Muscovado sugar

Finely grated zest and juice of
    ½ organic lemon

½ vanilla bean, split open and seeds
    scraped out

½ cinnamon stick

¼ cup (60 ml) water

For the custards:

2 ⅓ cups (550 ml) whole milk

1 vanilla bean, split open and seeds
    scraped out

4 cardamom pods, crushed

½ cinnamon stick

1 large egg plus 3 large egg yolks

¼ cup (50 g; 1 ¾ oz) blond cane
    sugar

If you walk into a French supermarket, you might be as amazed as Philip was the first time he saw the selection of yogurts, *crèmes desserts,* custards, and mousses in the refrigerated section. The French love anything creamy, like these *petits pots de crème.* My mother made a batch flavored with chocolate and vanilla at least once a week, and it was one of the simplest desserts that my brother and I enjoyed. To mine I have added the tart sweetness of applesauce and the delicious aroma of cardamom, making them even more scrumptious. Lulu absolutely adores these—and that started when she was only ten months old.

Note: Feel free to make these custards without the applesauce; and vary the spices used to infuse the milk as you please.

To make the applesauce: In a pot, combine all the ingredients. Bring to a simmer and cook over low heat for 25 minutes, or until the apples are soft. Remove the vanilla bean and cinnamon stick and, using a blender or food processor, purée the apples. Transfer to a bowl and let cool. Add 1 tablespoon of applesauce to the bottom of 6 glass jars; set aside. Note that you will have extra applesauce, which is delicious on its own or added to a yogurt.

To prepare the custards: Preheat the oven to 320°F (160°C) and prepare a water bath (see Basic Cooking Techniques, page 27, for instructions).

In a pot, combine the milk, vanilla bean and seeds, cardamom, and cinnamon stick. Bring to a gentle boil, making sure that it doesn't overflow, then remove from the heat and cover the pot. Leave to infuse for 30 minutes, then using a fine sieve or *chinois,* strain the milk. The milk should remain warm to the touch when you dip a finger in it; gently reheat it if necessary.

In the meantime, in a bowl, beat the egg and yolks with the sugar. Pour in the infused milk while stirring. Pour the milk mixture into the jars, making sure to discard any foam that might have formed on the surface.

Place the jars in the water bath, place in the oven, and cook for 45 to 50 minutes. The custards are ready when the cream is set (the middle might still be moving slightly when you jiggle the jars, and that's fine).

Let cool at room temperature, allowing the creams to set completely. Place a piece of plastic wrap on top of each and refrigerate for a few hours for the custards to completely set. Though I must confess that I personally like them when they are still slightly lukewarm; I can never resist. The creams keep, refrigerated, for 4 days.

Lavender île flottantes

Whenever I go back to France and have dinner in a low-key restaurant, if *île flottantes* (floating islands) are on the menu, it is, without a doubt, the dessert that I will order—to this day, it's still one of my favorites... anything with the word custard attached to it. Though magical in appearance, this dessert is far from complicated—it's simply composed of cooked whipped egg whites sitting on top of a flavored silky *crème anglaise*. In this recipe, lavender flowers impart a lovely flavor to the custard, but if you prefer something more traditional, you can use vanilla alone; or for a chocolate variant, add 3 ½ oz (100 g) grated dark chocolate to the custard when pouring the milk, and proceed in the same way. Likewise, you could substitute heavy cream for some of the milk to make the custard thicker and richer. I personally like the texture when it's made with milk only, but you won't be disappointed either way you make it.

Serves 4

2 ½ cups (600 ml) whole milk

1 teaspoon edible lavender
    flowers

1 vanilla bean, split open and seeds
    scraped out

4 large eggs, separated

⅓ cup (70 g; 2 ½ oz) blond cane
    sugar

Pinch of sea salt

Cocoa powder, to serve (optional)

In a pot, combine the milk with the lavender flowers and vanilla beans and seeds. Bring to a boil, making sure that it doesn't overflow, then remove from the heat. Cover the pot and leave to infuse for 1 hour or more. The longer you leave the milk to infuse, the more aromatic it will be—you could leave it a few hours or even overnight. Strain and reheat the milk until it's hot but not boiling.

In the meantime, in the bowl of a stand mixer, beat the egg yolks with three-quarters of the sugar until the mixture is pale in color. Pour the milk in slowly, stirring constantly. Transfer the custard back to the pot. Cook over medium-low heat, stirring constantly with a wooden spoon, and making sure it doesn't boil. It will take about 7 minutes for the custard to thicken, depending on the heat; it's ready when it coats the spoon. Divide the custard among 4 small dishes or 1 large dish and let cool, stirring occasionally.

To prepare the islands, which are basically a meringue, fill a pot with water and bring it to a simmer. Beat the egg whites with a pinch of sea salt until soft peaks form. When the egg whites form soft peaks, add the rest of the sugar and continue to beat for 1 minute, until the meringue is firm. Drop the whites into the simmering water ¼ cup at a time. Cook on each side for

30 to 45 seconds, turning the egg whites carefully with a slotted spoon. Once cooked, the texture should have firmed up. Remove with the slotted spoon and place on a paper towel to drain. Top the custards with the islands and place the dishes in the fridge for a few hours to set.

When you're ready to serve, dust with cocoa powder, if you like, although this is optional. Toasted nuts, like slivered almonds, are also a delicious addition.

Rice pudding

with strawberries stewed in lemongrass and lime

The words *rice pudding* have an extraordinary effect on every member of Philip's Irish family, most particularly his mother, Patricia. I still remember the day when she was visiting for a short weekend and I told her I had prepared rice pudding for dessert. Her eyes! They widened, instantly, lit with excitement, the way you see it happen with children standing in front of a piece of candy they want *now*! Dinner was hardly finished when she asked for dessert. "What is it about rice pudding that you like so much?" I could not help but ask her, amused when I saw she was licking the pot clean. "Papa and I *loved* to make rice pudding late at night," she answered, with a hint of emotion as she mentioned her late father's name. "Mother never understood!" But I did. Who could resist the flavor of warm beads of rice filled with a sweet milky juice?

This recipe suggests serving the rice pudding with a blend of stewed and fresh strawberries flavored with hints of lemongrass and ginger. But you should let your imagination and *gourmandise* guide you and vary the fruit according to the seasons: apple and pear in the fall; rhubarb and red berries in spring and summer; and adding toasted nuts if you like too.

Serves 4

2 lemongrass stalks

⅓ cup (40 g; 1 ½ oz) slivered
    almonds

1 pound (450 g) strawberries, hulled
    and diced

Finely grated zest of 1 ½ organic limes

Juice of 1 organic lime

¼ cup plus 2 tablespoons (75 g;
    2 ½ oz) blond cane sugar

2 tablespoons water

2 ⅓ cups (550 ml) whole milk

½ cup (100 g; 3 ½ oz) carnaroli rice,
    or another risotto rice

1-inch piece fresh ginger, peeled

¼ cup (60 ml) unsweetened
    coconut milk

Remove the thicker outer layer of the lemongrass stalks and chop them. Using a coffee grinder or spice grinder, very finely grind the white thicker part of 1 lemongrass stalk; set aside. Slice the other stalk into 3 pieces; set aside.

Toast the slivered almonds in a frying pan over medium heat for about 3 to 4 minutes, or until lightly browned and fragrant; set aside to cool.

In a small pot, combine 10 oz (280 g) of the strawberries with the zest of 1 lime, 1 teaspoon of ground lemongrass, 2 tablespoons of the sugar, and the water. Bring to a boil, then reduce the heat and simmer for 5 minutes, or until the strawberries soften but still keep their shape. Remove from the heat and add the lime juice; set aside to cool.

In the meantime, rinse the rice under cold water. In a pot, combine the milk with the 3 lemongrass slices, the ginger, and zest of ½ lime; bring to a boil, making sure that it doesn't overflow. When it reaches the boiling point, pour the rice in slowly and lower the heat. Simmer for 30 minutes, stirring regularly until the rice is soft and creamy. Discard the lemongrass and ginger and stir in the remaining ¼ cup sugar and the coconut milk—most of the liquid will be absorbed. Transfer the rice to a bowl and let cool slightly. It's best eaten lukewarm.

In a bowl, gently combine the cooked strawberries with the fresh ones. Divide the rice pudding among 4 bowls and top with the strawberries and slivered almonds.

Chocolate and plum almond cake

with cinnamon

I should tell you that the pairing of dark chocolate, almonds, and plums inside this cake makes it absolutely spectacular. And it looks beautiful too, when the cake is baked in a rectangular mold so that each piece of fruit is shown off in a slice. Over time, I've baked many variations—some with sweet rice flour replacing amaranth flour; nectarines, apples, or apricots replacing the plums—each never failing to please our tastebuds.

Preheat the oven to 350°F (180°C). Butter the mold and line it with parchment paper; set aside.

In a frying pan, melt 2 tablespoons of the butter over medium heat. Add the plum slices along with 2 tablespoons of the sugar and the cinnamon. Cook for 2 minutes on each side; remove from the heat and set aside.

Melt the chocolate with 6 tablespoons of the butter in a bain-marie (see Basic Cooking Techniques, page 27, for instructions); set aside.

In a bowl, combine the almond meal, amaranth flour, sea salt, baking powder, and baking soda; set aside.

In the bowl of a stand mixer, beat the eggs with ⅓ cup sugar until the batter is light and pale in color. Stir in the vanilla, then the melted chocolate and the flour mixture, until just combined. Pour the cake batter into the mold and arrange the slices of plums on top. Place the cake in the oven and bake for 25 minutes, or until the blade of a knife inserted in the middle comes out dry. Remove from the oven and let cool before unmolding. Dust with confectioners' sugar and slice between the plums to serve.

Serves 4 to 6

You will need: a 13-¾-by-4-½-inch springform mold, or, if you prefer, you can use a different shape mold, or even bake the cake in individual molds

6 tablespoons (90 g; 3 oz) unsalted butter, plus 1 tablespoon for the plums and more for the mold

2 red plums, pitted and sliced (or substitute apples, apricots, or nectarines according to the season)

⅓ cup (70 g; 2 ½ oz) blond cane sugar, plus 2 tablespoons for the plums

¼ teaspoon ground cinnamon

2 oz (60 g; 2 oz) dark chocolate (64% cocoa content)

⅔ cup (80 g; 2 ¾ oz) almond meal

⅓ cup (50 g; 1 ¾ oz) amaranth flour

Pinch of sea salt

½ teaspoon baking powder

½ teaspoon baking soda

2 large eggs

½ teaspoon pure vanilla extract

Confectioners' sugar, to dust

Baked apples
with spices, olive oil, and nuts

Apple picking in the fall is a food tradition I've grown up with, and one that I wait for impatiently every year. In the French village where my parents live, everyone has at least one or two apple trees in their back garden, and if not, they have a friend who has one. So I am quite fond of, and also picky about, the taste of an apple.

I find that baking apples is one of the simplest yet most delicious ways to enjoy them as a dessert, especially when I can find good heirloom varieties. Always a treat. With this recipe, the pairing of the lemony apple juice flavored with hints of vanilla and olive oil is so tasty that Philip and I will slurp it up by the spoonful.

Serves 4

4 tablespoons dried cranberries,
    finely chopped

4 tablespoons shelled unsalted green
    pistachios, finely chopped

4 tablespoons slivered almonds,
    finely chopped

1 cup (235 ml) fresh apple juice or
    light apple cider

Finely grated zest and juice of
    1 organic lemon

1 vanilla bean, split open and seeds
    scraped out

4 apples, such as Reinette, pink lady,
    Cortland, Winesap, or Liberty

4 cinnamon sticks

3 tablespoons olive oil

2 tablespoons turbinado sugar

In a small bowl, combine the cranberries, pistachios, and almonds; set aside.

In a pot, combine the apple juice, lemon zest, vanilla bean and seeds. Bring to a boil, then remove from the heat. Cover and leave to infuse for 30 minutes.

Preheat the oven to 350°F (180°C).

Core the apples, then slice the top off of each one (set them aside) and drizzle with lemon juice. Place the apples in a baking dish and divide the nut-cranberry stuffing among them. Place a cinnamon stick in each apple and cover them with their tops. Pour the infused juice and the oil over the apples and sprinkle with sugar.

Place the apples in the oven and bake for 1 hour, or until the flesh is tender, regularly drizzling with the cooking juice. Remove from the oven and serve warm with the juices and plain yogurt on the side.

When it comes to pistachios, I like to use the Iranian or Sicilian varieties for their exceptional green color.

A LOVE FOR FRUIT

"Ce sont les premières, goûte!" ("They are the first of the season, try!")
my mother told me when she put in my hand two small strawberries that she'd picked from the garden earlier that morning — *des fraises gariguette* (small strawberries commonly found
in France in early May, at the start of the season). They were
irregular in shape and covered in dirt from the heavy rain of
the previous night, but I knew that underneath that misleading
cover, I would find something extremely tasty and juicy.

"Oh là là, que c'est bon!" ("Oh, it's so good!") I exclaimed, eager
for more. The flavor was so concentrated that for a moment, I
felt like the essence of strawberry had perfumed my mouth.

I grew up surrounded by *les fruits rouges* (red berries). It's one
of the many privileges of living in the countryside, besides wak-
ing up to the next-door neighbor's rooster. There is green
space, wild flowers in the fields, orchards, and fruit trees; it's
the best playground I can imagine. There were even cows, goats,
and chickens for my delight. I am sure my parents and brother,
who still live there, forget how lucky they are to have it all, so
close and accessible. At the back of their houses, strawberries,
red currants, rhubarb, raspberries, and apple, pear, and cherry
trees grow like weeds.

Given this abundance of fruit, making preserves was something we thrived on at home. We'd follow the seasons, watching the fruit, discussing statistics of how well the crop was going to be each season—waiting for the fruit to be ready. In early spring, rhubarb showed its pretty pink face. When June came, juicy cherries, strawberries, and raspberries kept us busy, soon followed in July by brightly colored red currants. In August, we'd buy boxes of delicious aromatic nectarines and apricots shipped from southern France where the sun is warm enough to ripen these fruits—and with them, we'd prepare cute little jars of jam. In September, apples, pears, and plums came in numbers. We'd make *fruits au sirop* (fruit preserved in syrup) and bake tarts and *clafoutis*. It was hard to keep up, but friends, neighbors, and family were always happy to leave our house with a few buckets full of sweet juicy jewels. Then the next year we'd start all over again, comparing the new season's crop to the past one.

I haven't lost this fruit habit, and I'm still fond of using them in my desserts, celebrating each season with the best fruit that it bears. Besides being delicious, they are also irresistibly cute. Don't you think so too?

Pretty pink lady apple tartlets

with ginger, lemon, and walnuts

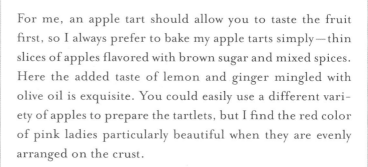

For me, an apple tart should allow you to taste the fruit first, so I always prefer to bake my apple tarts simply — thin slices of apples flavored with brown sugar and mixed spices. Here the added taste of lemon and ginger mingled with olive oil is exquisite. You could easily use a different variety of apples to prepare the tartlets, but I find the red color of pink ladies particularly beautiful when they are evenly arranged on the crust.

Makes six 5-inch tartlets

You will need: a 5-inch cookie cutter or ring mold

Lemon-flavored olive oil crust (see
  Basic Recipes, page 21)
1 ¾ oz (50 g) walnuts
4 tablespoons light Muscovado sugar
1-inch piece fresh ginger, peeled and
  finely grated
Finely grated zest of 1 large lemon
2 to 3 red apples, like pink lady or
  Honeycrisp, cored and sliced
  thinly, drizzled with lemon juice
  to prevent discoloration
Drizzle of lemon juice
3 tablespoons honey
3 tablespoons olive oil

Preheat the oven to 400°F (200°C) and cover a baking sheet with parchment paper; set aside.

Roll out each ball of dough, and using a 5-inch cookie cutter or ring mold with a sharp edge, cut the crust into 3 circles. Repeat with the other balls of crust, also reusing the leftovers until you have 6 circles in total. Make small holes in them with a fork. Place them on your baking sheet and refrigerate, covered with a piece of parchment, while you prepare the rest of the tart.

Place the walnuts in the bowl of a food processor and grind them into a fine powder. Transfer to a bowl and add the sugar, ginger, and lemon zest. Divide this sugary mixture evenly over the crusts, leaving a ½-inch border at the edges free of the sugar mixture. Arrange the apple slices on top so that they cover the crust entirely. Drizzle with lemon juice. Heat the honey in a small pot and brush the slices of apple with it, then with the olive oil.

Place the tartlets in the oven and bake for 25 minutes, or until they are golden on top. Using a spatula, transfer them to a cooling rack and let cool completely before serving. Serve with a scoop of vanilla ice cream if you want.

Apricot tartlets

with honey, almonds, and olive oil

This recipe is a variation on the previous apple tartlet recipe. In the summer, why not substitute apricots and almond meal for the apples and walnuts? These tartlets are a favorite for their wholesome, juicy, summery sweetness. Make sure to buy apricots that are fully ripe, as the result will be incomparable.

Preheat the oven to 400°F (200°C).

Roll and cut the dough to fit inside the tartlet molds (use the leftovers to make more tartlets, or keep for another time). Arrange the dough inside each mold and using a fork, make small holes at the bottom. Refrigerate, covered with a piece of parchment paper, while you prepare the fruit.

In a bowl, combine the almond meal, sugar, and lime zest. Take the molds out of the fridge and divide the sugar-nut mixture among the tartlets. Arrange the slices of apricots on top and add red currants, if using. Drizzle evenly with the honey and oil.

Place the tartlets in the oven and bake for 25 to 30 minutes, until the crust is golden in color and the apricots are soft and have released their juice. Remove from the oven and let cool before serving.

Makes four 4 ½-inch tartlets

You will need: four 4 ½-inch tartlet molds

Lemon-flavored olive oil crust (see Basic Recipes, page 21), or millet, amaranth, and brown rice crust (see Basic Recipes, page 23)

6 to 8 ripe apricots (about 2 per tartlet, according to size), pitted and sliced

4 tablespoons almond meal (or 4 tablespoons shelled unsalted green pistachios, finely ground)

2 tablespoons blond cane sugar

Finely grated zest of 1 organic lime

¼ cup red currants (optional)

2 tablespoons honey

2 tablespoons olive oil

Spiced panna cotta
with raspberries

"We brought you dessert," my mother-in-law exclaimed as she walked into our room. It was December 26 and on Christmas day, I had just given birth to our beautiful baby girl, Lulu.

Philip and I looked exhausted but were beaming with joy! And me, with curiosity about the dessert. "What is it?" I asked, intrigued. "I found them in your fridge," she replied, holding a plate with two glasses filled with *panna cotta.*

Oh yes, I remembered now! The *panna cotta* that I had made the day I went into labor. I had a good excuse for having forgotten! But now that they were here, in front of me, all I could think was that I *really* wanted a taste. The texture of the cream was so soft and light that it felt as if it were disappearing in my mouth. I looked up and smiled. "Thank you for bringing them!" I said, happy as can be with my new baby. And with the delicious taste of the dessert lingering in my mouth.

Note: I prefer the texture of panna cotta *to have a melt-in-the mouth feel. Hence, I add as little gelatin as is necessary for the cream to hold its shape. Serve it with stewed and fresh raspberries, like here, or add another fruit, like diced apples sauteed in butter, sugar, and vanilla seeds. Or just eat it plain.*

Serves 4

For the raspberry sauce:
14 oz (400 g) raspberries, or any
    mixed berries of your choice
4 tablespoons blond cane sugar
2 teaspoons cornstarch

For the *panna cotta:*
2 ½ gelatin sheets (5 g; .17 oz), or
    1 ¼ teaspoons gelatin powder
2 cups (475 ml) half-and-half, or you
    can use 1 cup whole milk and 1 cup
    heavy cream
¼ cup (50 g; 1 ¾ oz) blond cane sugar
1 vanilla bean, split open and seeds
    scraped out
6 cardamom pods, crushed

To prepare the raspberry sauce: In a pot, combine 12 oz of the raspberries with the sugar. Bring to a bare boil, then reduce the heat and simmer until the fruit softens. Stir in the cornstarch. Remove from the heat, strain, and let cool slightly. Divide three-quarters of this raspberry sauce into the bottom of 4 glasses. In a bowl, combine the remainder of the sauce with the rest of the raspberries; refrigerate until ready to use.

To prepare the *panna cotta:* Soak the gelatin sheets in a large bowl of cold water for 5 to 10 minutes.

In the meantime, pour the half-and-half into a pot. Warm over medium heat and add the sugar, vanilla seeds and bean, and cardamom. Bring to a bare simmer and simmer for 4 minutes. Remove from the heat, cover, and leave to infuse for 20 minutes. Discard the vanilla bean and cardamom pods, and reheat the cream slightly if it has cooled too much—it should feel warm to the touch when dipping a finger into it.

Using your fingertips, squeeze out the excess water from the gelatin sheets. Add them to the warm cream and stir until they dissolve.

Pouring slowly, divide the cream among the prepared glasses. Let cool and refrigerate for at least 4 hours, or overnight. Top with the raspberry sauce and the rest of the raspberries and serve.

Apple, rhubarb, and strawberry nutty crumble

It's not difficult to become a crumble lover—the dessert, a crisp nutty topping that encloses warm pieces of fruit stewing in their own juice is simply irresistible. Especially when it's served with vanilla-flavored custard, just the way Billy, Philip's Irish grandfather, used to eat it. We feel proud to be prolonging the family tradition.

Serves 6 to 8

You will need: eight 8-oz ramekins or a 10-by-7-inch baking dish

For the fruit:
4 rhubarb stalks (350 g; 12 ½ oz), peeled and diced
2 large McIntosh or Cortland apples, peeled, cored, and diced
9 oz (255 g) strawberries, hulled and diced

1 teaspoon lemon extract
¼ cup (50 g; 1 ¾ oz) blond cane sugar
Finely grated zest of 1 organic orange
Unsalted butter, for the ramekins

For the nut crumble:
⅓ cup (40 g; 1 ½ oz) hazelnut flour
⅓ cup (55 g; 2 oz) sweet rice flour
⅓ cup (40 g; 1 ½ oz) millet flour or amaranth flour
½ packed cup (100 g; 3 ½ oz) light Muscovado sugar

1 ½ oz (40 g) walnuts, coarsely chopped
1 oz (30 g) shelled unsalted green pistachios, coarsely chopped
⅓ cup (35 g; 1 ¼ oz) rolled oats
6 tablespoons (85 g; 3 oz) unsalted butter, diced, at room temperature

Plain yogurt or *crème anglaise* (see Basic Recipes, page 26), to serve

To prepare the fruit: In a bowl, combine the fruit with the lemon extract, sugar, and orange zest; let rest for 30 minutes. Butter eight 1-cup ramekins; set aside.

To prepare the nut crumble: In a bowl, combine the hazelnut, sweet rice, and millet flours, the sugar, walnuts, pistachios, and rolled oats. Add the butter and, using your fingertips, work until coarse crumbles form; cover and refrigerate until ready to use.

Preheat the oven to 350°F (180°C).

Divide the fruit among the ramekins and top with the crumble. Bake the crumbles for 30 to 35 minutes, until the fruit bubbles and the topping is golden. Remove from the oven, let cool slightly, and serve with plain yogurt or *crème anglaise*.

Cherry clafoutis

with an exotic flair

If Philip had to choose a few desserts to take with him to a desert island, a *clafoutis* would be one of them. It's the dessert he ate at my parents' house the first time we visited them together. And I think that it's also the dessert that convinced him that he had to marry me. Traditionally, a *clafoutis* (pronounced like kla-foo-TEE) is a vanilla-flavored pudding-like dessert studded with cherries—best eaten at room temperature—but many other types of fruit are possible. I personally have a weakness for a *clafoutis* baked with juicy sun-ripened apricots—so pretty too—plums, or strawberries and rhubarb. This recipe offers an exotic twist, as the cherries are baked with coconut milk and lime, a truly winning pairing!

Note: For a more traditional clafoutis, *replace the coconut milk with heavy cream, the cornstarch, millet flour, and almond meal with ¾ cup all-purpose flour, and omit the lime. That was, and still is, the French* clafoutis *my mother baked for us.*

Serves 6

You will need: one 12-inch mold or six 8-oz ramekins

Unsalted butter, for the mold
½ cup (100 g; 3 ½ oz) blond cane sugar, plus more to sprinkle the mold(s)
¾ cup plus 2 tablespoons (200 ml) whole milk

¾ cup plus 2 tablespoons (200 ml) unsweetened coconut milk or heavy cream
Finely grated zest of 1 small organic lime
1 vanilla bean, split open and seeds scraped out
3 large eggs

⅓ cup (40 g; 1 ¾ oz) millet flour
¼ cup (30 g; 1 oz) almond meal
¼ cup (30 g; 1 oz) cornstarch
2 tablespoons melted unsalted butter
1 pound 5 ¼ oz (600 g) ripe sweet or sour cherries (such as Rainier or Bing)
Confectioners' sugar, to dust

Preheat the oven to 350°F (180°C). Butter a 12-inch mold, or six 8-oz cup ramekins, and sprinkle with sugar; tap the excess out.

In a small pot, heat the milk and coconut milk with the lime zest and vanilla seeds and bean. Turn off the heat, cover, and let it infuse for 15 minutes. Strain and set aside.

In a bowl, combine the sugar, millet flour, almond meal, and cornstarch. Beat in the eggs, one at a time. Stir in the infused milk and melted butter. Arrange the cherries in the mold or ramekins and pour the batter on top.

Place the *clafoutis* in the oven and bake for 35 to 40 minutes—25 to 30 minutes if you're using ramekins—until the flan is set and golden in color. Remove from the oven and let cool to room temperature. Dust with confectioners' sugar and serve.

The French like to debate whether the cherry pits should be left in or not for a **clafoutis**. Those who believe they should be left in will tell you that they impart an additional flavor. It's something I tend to agree with, even if it's subtle. Besides, spitting the pits out is always fun to do — as kids, my brother and I turned this into a game. But you can always pit the cherries first if you prefer, which makes the eating part easier.

Blackberry tartlets
with vanilla-flavored mascarpone cream

There are beautiful-looking desserts that take a lot of time to prepare and others that don't—like these tartlets, which are prepared in a snap and look outstanding. Prepare the crust, mascarpone cream, and fruit stewed in syrup ahead of time. Then assemble the dessert at the last minute, when you're ready to serve, so it's fresh as can be—particularly convenient if other parts of dinner require more time. It's a dessert in which the flavors remain perfectly simple and refreshing.

To prepare the light syrup: In a small pot, combine the sugar, water, and vanilla bean and seeds and place over low heat. Heat, stirring gently, until the sugar dissolves. Add the blackberries and simmer for 4 minutes, or until the syrup colors from the fruit stewing in it. Remove from the heat and leave the blackberries to cool in the syrup.

Preheat the oven to 350°F (180°C). Roll and cut the dough to fit inside the tartlet molds. Arrange the dough inside each mold and using a fork, make small holes at the bottom. Prebake for 12 minutes (see Basic Cooking Techniques, page 27, for instructions). Remove the parchment paper and weights, and continue to bake for 5 minutes, watching carefully to make sure that the crusts do not brown too quickly. Unmold and let them cool on a rack.

To prepare the topping: In a bowl, beat the *mascarpone* with the sugar and vanilla seeds. In a separate bowl, beat the heavy cream with an electric mixer until it forms soft peaks. Fold it gently into the *mascarpone* mixture.

Just before you're ready to serve, assemble the tartlets by spreading the cream into the crusts. Top with the cooked blackberries and drizzle with syrup. Serve immediately.

Makes four 4½-inch tartlets

You will need: four 4½-inch tartlet molds

For the light syrup and blackberries:

2 tablespoons water

¼ cup (50 g; 1¾ oz) blond cane sugar

½ vanilla bean, split open and seeds scraped out

1 pound (450 g) blackberries

Rustic vanilla and amaranth sweet crust (see Basic Recipes, page 22)

For the topping:

9 oz (255 g) mascarpone cheese

4 tablespoons blond cane sugar

½ vanilla bean, split open and seeds scraped out

½ cup (120 ml) cold heavy cream

Raspberry, lime, and coconut milk creams

> If you like desserts with a tang, then these lime-flavored creams are for you. Not only because the dessert is full of zest, but also because it's quick to prepare and looks gorgeous when served in a glass.

Serves 4

You will need: four small glasses or ramekins

Unsalted butter, for the
    ramekins
7 oz (200 g) raspberries
2 large eggs
⅓ cup (80 g; 2 ¾ oz) blond cane
    sugar
Juice and finely grated zest of
    1 organic lime
1 ½ tablespoons butter, melted
1 cup (235 ml) unsweetened
    coconut milk
2 tablespoons almond meal
2 tablespoons cornstarch
Confectioners' sugar, to dust
    (optional)

Preheat the oven to 350°F (180°C).

Butter 4 glasses (such as small 1-cup water glasses) or ramekins and arrange three-quarters of the raspberries in the bottoms of them.

In a bowl, beat the eggs with the sugar until well incorporated. Stir in the lime zest and juice, the melted butter, and coconut milk. Beat in the almond meal and cornstarch. Divide this lime cream among the glasses and add the rest of the raspberries.

Place the creams in the oven and bake for 25 minutes, or until the flan is set. Let cool and serve at room temperature, dusted with confectioners' sugar, if using.

EVERYDAY BAKING

I am fond of the days when the first thing I do is bake a simple cake. I'll start gathering the ingredients and setting myself to work early in the morning, and usually the cake will be baked before Philip leaves for work, Lulu is awake, and our day gets too busy. Cautiously, I'll leave it to cool on the kitchen island.

Often I choose a cake with dark chocolate and nuts, like toasted pieces of walnuts; or sometimes I prefer to add pureed squash and spices to the batter; or perhaps slices of seasonal fruit. Every single one of these cakes is unpretentious but flavorful, never too sweet, but just enough to be enticing: the perfect balance of flavors. Some days I'll bake a loaf, or I'll divide it up into cute muffin-size cakes that are easy to take on-the-go or add to Lulu's lunch box. The aromas of sugar and chocolate, spices, or fruit baking in the oven always fill the house, making my stomach grumble just after breakfast. I *try* to forget about it, *le gâteau* (the cake), and I might be successful for a few hours when I'm behaving, but as the smell of the cake lingers, I often find myself drawn to the kitchen again like a magnet. *I'll just have a small piece,* I tell myself, *just to see whether I like it.* I cut a thin slice and hold it between my fingers to admire its moist texture and color. The cake stares back at me. *"C'mon, just do it,"* it's telling

me. I put the kettle on for a cup of rooibos or jasmine green tea, and sit at the dining table, my mouth already full with the first bite. *Oh, pas mal!* (not bad!) I think. *Maybe I'll have just a tiny bit more.*

My everyday cake. It's the one that I keep for our snacks during the day; the cake that makes us feel at home. And when it is gone, another cake comes to replace it. On that same corner of our kitchen island.

Lemongrass and blackberry teacakes

These are what my mother-in-law would call the perfect kind of teacakes—as an Irish woman, she knows! They are studded with blackberries and flavored with a hint of lemongrass, which gives them an unusual touch. Moist and divine! Feel free to substitute other berries of your choice for the blackberries—raspberries or red currants work well too. You can also use all-purpose flour in place of the rice flour, if that's what you have handy.

Makes 4 teacakes (large muffin size)

You will need: 4 rigid mini brioche or large muffin molds

5 tablespoons (70 g; 2 ½ oz) unsalted butter, plus more for molds

¼ cup (45 g; 1 ½ oz) white rice flour

½ cup (60 g; 2 oz) almond meal, sifted

½ cup (60 g; 2 oz) confectioners' sugar, sifted

Pinch of sea salt

¼ teaspoon baking powder

1 vanilla bean, split open and seeds scraped out

1 lemongrass stalk, finely chopped

2 large egg whites, lightly beaten until foamy

⅔ cup (100 g; 3 ½ oz) blackberries

Preheat the oven to 350°F (180°C). Butter 4 rigid mini brioche or large muffin molds; set aside.

Melt the butter in a small pot and set aside.

In a bowl, combine the rice flour, almond meal, confectioners' sugar, sea salt, and baking powder. Mix in the vanilla seeds and lemongrass. Make a hole in the middle of the dry ingredients and pour the egg whites into it. Mix together until smooth. Stir in the melted butter, then gently fold in the blackberries. Divide the batter among the molds.

Place in the oven and bake for 30 minutes, or until the blade of a sharp knife inserted in the middle comes out dry. Remove from the heat and let cool for a few minutes, then unmold the cakes onto a cooling rack. The cakes will keep for a few days wrapped in plastic in the fridge and then slightly reheated in the oven or microwave.

Banana, chocolate, and hazelnut muffins

Makes 12 muffins

1 ½ oz (40 g) hazelnuts or walnuts

2 large eggs

½ cup (100 g; 3 ½ oz) blond cane
    sugar

8 tablespoons (113 g; 4 oz) unsalted
    butter, melted

¼ cup plain whole yogurt

½ cup (70 g; 2 ½ oz) buckwheat
    flour

1 cup (120 g; 4 ¼ oz) quinoa flour

½ cup (60 g; 2 oz) hazelnut flour

Pinch of sea salt

1 teaspoon baking powder

½ teaspoon baking soda

3 ripe bananas, mashed with a fork

3 oz (90 g) dark chocolate (70%
    cocoa), coarsely chopped

"Why don't you freeze some?" Patricia asked when she saw the muffins I'd baked cooling on the countertop. *Genius!* I thought. I liked her idea because it meant that I could enjoy something sweet at any time of the day, whenever a sudden muffin craving hit me. These muffins are decadent and extremely moist, showing off the delicious flavors of banana, dark chocolate, buckwheat, and hazelnut—always a winning combination in my eyes.

Note: If you freeze some of the muffins, reheat them for 1 minute in the microwave, or for a few more minutes if you use a toaster oven or an oven preheated to 300°F (150°C). They'll be as if they were coming fresh out of the oven. Think about all of that melting chocolate . . .

Toast the hazelnuts in a frying pan over medium heat for about 4 to 5 minutes, or until lightly browned and fragrant. Place them in a clean kitchen towel and rub them to remove the skins. When they are cool enough to be handled, chop them coarsely; set aside.

Preheat the oven to 350°F (180°C). Line a muffin pan with 12 paper liners, or use silicone muffin molds.

In the bowl of a stand mixer, beat the eggs with the sugar until light and pale in color. Stir in the melted butter and the yogurt. In another bowl, combine the flours, salt, baking powder, and baking soda. Stir the dry ingredients into the egg mixture, until just combined. Add the bananas, hazelnuts, and chopped chocolate, and mix gently.

Divide the batter among the muffin holes, place in the oven, and bake for 25 to 30 minutes, until the blade of a sharp knife inserted in the middle of the muffins comes out almost dry. Remove from the oven and let cool briefly, then invert onto a cooling rack to cool completely.

Brown butter pistachio and poppy seed financiers

A *financier* is a French cake typically made with brown butter and almond meal. This recipe is a twist on the original, with my own touches: rice flour and green pistachios to replace the almond meal, cardamom to give a delicious flavor to the batter, and the use of muffin paper liners instead of the special *financier* mold. In the end, it does not matter what you decide to call the cakes—the important thing is that they are really beautiful and scrumptious.

Makes 8 muffin-size financiers

½ cup (90 g; 3 oz) shelled unsalted green pistachios

7 tablespoons (100 g; 3 ½ oz) unsalted butter

5 cardamom pods, crushed

1 vanilla bean, split open and seeds scraped out

⅓ cup (60 g; 2 oz) white rice flour

2 tablespoons poppy seeds

½ cup (100 g; 3 ½ oz) blond cane sugar

½ teaspoon sea salt

4 large egg whites, beaten lightly until foamy

Preheat the oven to 350°F (180°C). Line a muffin pan with 8 paper liners, or use silicone muffin molds; set aside.

Using a coffee or spice grinder, grind the pistachios into a fine powder; set aside.

In a small pot, melt the butter over medium heat until it turns light brown in color; remove from the heat. Add the cardamom pods and vanilla bean and seeds and let rest for 10 minutes; strain and set aside.

In a bowl, combine the rice flour, pistachio powder, poppy seeds, sugar, and salt. Beat in the egg whites until smooth, and then stir in the melted butter, making sure to work quickly.

Divide the batter among the muffin cases, place the *financiers* in the oven, and bake for 20 minutes, or until a knife inserted in the middle of a cake comes out dry. Remove from the oven and let cool completely.

If you prefer, you can make mini financiers *using a mini muffin pan lined with mini muffin paper cases, something I did for Lulu's first birthday party. In this case, the recipe will make 24 of them. Fill each mold with a heaping tablespoon and bake for 12 to 14 minutes.*

Red kuri squash muffins

Makes 10 muffins

2 large eggs

½ cup (100 g; 3 ½ oz) blond cane
    sugar

7 tablespoons (100 g; 3 ½ oz)
    unsalted butter, melted

¾ cup (200 g; 7 oz) puréed red kuri
    squash or butternut squash

1 teaspoon grated fresh ginger

½ cup (60 g; 2 oz) quinoa flour
    or millet flour

¼ cup (35 g; 1 ¼ oz) amaranth flour

¼ cup (40 g; 1 ½ oz) sweet rice flour

Pinch of sea salt

1 teaspoon baking powder

½ teaspoon baking soda

1 teaspoon ground cinnamon

¼ teaspoon freshly grated
    nutmeg

For the frosting (optional):

8 oz (225 g) *mascarpone* cheese, at
    room temperature

4 tablespoons (60 g; 2 oz) unsalted
    butter, softened

1 teaspoon pure vanilla extract

¼ cup (30 g; 1 oz) confectioners'
    sugar, sifted

¼ cup (60 ml) maple syrup

I baked these spiced squash muffins for a Halloween brunch Philip and I were invited to. When we arrived at our friends David and Kumi's apartment and Kumi opened the front door in her sweatpants, we suddenly realized that something wasn't right.

"Brunch was yesterday!" Kumi exclaimed, with a smile.

We stared at each other and laughed. How could we have come on the wrong day?

"Come on in," she added cheerfully. "The house is still a mess, so don't pay attention!"

"Well, I brought you muffins!" I responded, handing her the small bag of muffins.

We sat down around the kitchen table and Kumi made a pot of warm tea. We were so happy to catch up that, while Lulu and their baby daughter, Ruby, played on the mat, we chatted for perhaps three hours, maybe more. And somehow, the plate of muffins slowly emptied, without a single crumb left.

These muffins can also be dressed up for a special occasion by frosting them. The simple maple-flavored *mascarpone* frosting is included here for this purpose, but it's optional—the muffins are delicious either way.

Preheat the oven to 350°F (180°C). Line a muffin pan with 10 paper liners, or use silicone muffin molds; set aside.

In the bowl of a stand mixer, beat the eggs with the sugar until light and pale in color. Reduce the speed and beat in the melted butter, puréed squash, and ginger.

In a separate bowl, combine the flours with the sea salt, baking powder, baking soda, and spices. Mix the dry ingredients into the squash mixture using a spatula.

Divide the batter among the muffin cases, place in the oven, and bake for 25 minutes, or until a knife inserted in the middle comes out dry. Remove from the oven and let cool briefly, then invert onto a rack to cool completely.

To prepare the frosting: Using an electric hand mixer or a stand mixer, beat the *mascarpone* and butter until well combined. Stir in the vanilla and, while beating, gradually add the sugar and then the maple syrup.

Spoon the frosting into a pastry bag fitted with the tip of your choice and frost the muffins. Enjoy right away, or refrigerate to help the frosting to set. (If you refrigerate the muffins, take them out 30 minutes or so before eating—they taste best at room temperature.)

To prepare the squash purée, there are two possible methods: roasting or steaming. First, slice the squash open and remove the seeds. If you're using red kuri squash, there is no need to peel it. To roast, preheat the oven to 350°F (180°C). Cut the squash into smaller slices and place them on a baking sheet. Bake the squash for 45 minutes, or until the flesh is soft; purée in a food processor. To steam the squash, place the pieces of squash in a steamer basket over simmering water and steam for about 15 minutes, until fork-tender; purée in a food processor or with a ricer.

Buckwheat and almond chocolate cake

The issue I have with chocolate cakes is that I always find a new recipe that makes me more enthusiastic and thinking, "this one is the best chocolate cake I've ever made!" It's not a bad thing, as Philip and I are true chocolate cake lovers. This cake was improvised one summer day, when Lulu and I were home and, despite the heat, I desperately felt the urge to eat a slice of chocolate cake. I liked its moist texture so much that during the weeks that followed, I kept making it over and over again. I think you might enjoy it too, as much as we do.

Preheat the oven to 350°F (180°C). Cut a round piece of parchment paper large enough to cover the sides and bottom of the mold. Butter the mold and line it with the parchment paper; set aside.

Place the butter and chocolate in a bowl and melt it in a bain-marie (see Basic Cooking Techniques, page 27, for instructions).

In the bowl of a stand mixer, beat the eggs with the sugar and sea salt until light and pale in color and the batter has doubled in volume. Gently fold in the vanilla and the melted chocolate mixture. Sprinkle the flour and almond meal over the batter and fold gently to combine.

Pour the batter into the cake mold, place in the oven, and bake for 30 minutes, or until the blade of a sharp knife inserted in the middle comes out dry. Remove from the oven, let cool for 5 minutes, then flip it gently onto a plate. Remove the parchment paper carefully and flip again—the top part will crack and might look a bit messy, but that's normal as the cake rises and falls slightly. Dust with confectioners' sugar and serve at room temperature.

Makes one 9-inch round cake

You will need: a 9-inch round cake mold

7 tablespoons (100 g; 3 ½ oz) unsalted butter, plus more for the mold

3 ½ oz (100 g) bittersweet dark chocolate (70% cocoa)

4 large eggs, at room temperature

½ cup (100 g; 3 ½ oz) blond cane sugar

Pinch of sea salt

1 teaspoon pure vanilla extract

¼ cup (35 g; 1 ¼ oz) buckwheat flour

¼ cup (30 g; 1 oz) almond meal

Confectioners' sugar, to serve

Upside down cranberry cake
with olive oil, vanilla, and saffron

Makes one 9-inch round cake

You will need: a 9-inch round
cake mold

For the cranberry topping:

1 tablespoon (14 g; ½ oz)
    butter

3 cups (300 g; 10 ½ oz) fresh
    cranberries

2 tablespoons blond cane sugar

For the cake batter:

½ cup plain whole yogurt

½ cup (100 g; 3½ oz) blond cane
    sugar

⅓ cup olive oil

1 vanilla bean, split open and seeds
    scraped out

¼ teaspoon saffron threads

3 large eggs

½ cup (60 g; 2 oz) quinoa flour or
    millet flour

½ cup (90 g; 3 oz) brown rice flour

⅓ cup (40 g; 1 ½ oz) almond meal

2 tablespoons cornstarch

2 teaspoons baking powder

½ teaspoon baking soda

Pinch of sea salt

I didn't discover cranberries until I moved to the United States, as we don't grow them in France. I fell in love right away, with an eager curiosity for finding new ways to use them—like in this recipe: an original upside down cake that combines the rich flavors of olive oil, vanilla, and saffron with the tartness of cranberries. Utterly surprising, exotic—and moist!

Note: This cake is also excellent with apples. Use 2 apples. Core and slice them. Saute on each side with butter and sugar for 2 minutes. Then arrange them at the bottom of the parchment-paper-lined dish.

Preheat the oven to 350°F (180°C). Cut a round piece of parchment paper large enough to cover the sides and bottom of the cake mold. Butter the cake mold and line it with the parchment paper; set aside.

To prepare the cranberry topping: In a pot, melt the butter over medium heat. Add the cranberries and sugar and cook for a few minutes, stirring occasionally until the cranberries soften slightly. Transfer the cranberries to the cake mold, spreading them to cover the bottom entirely.

To prepare the cake batter: In a large bowl, beat the yogurt with the sugar. Stir in the olive oil, vanilla seeds, saffron, and eggs.

In a separate bowl, combine the quinoa and brown rice flours, the almond meal, cornstarch, baking powder, baking soda, and sea salt. Add the dry ingredients to the wet and mix thoroughly, taking care not to overwork the batter.

Pour the batter over the cranberries, place in the oven, and bake for 30 to 35 minutes, until the blade of a knife inserted in the cake comes out dry. Carefully flip the cake onto a plate and let cool slightly before removing the parchment paper. Serve with plain yogurt or whipped cream.

Chocolate tahini cookies

Cookies sneaked into my kitchen when I met Philip. You see, since I didn't grow up in a culture where cookies are prominent baked goods—I grew up on fruit tarts instead—it took time before cookies grew on me and I would eventually think, "How could I have *ever* lived without cookies before?" Whenever we go hiking and bring a picnic, if I don't pack muffins, then we'll definitely have a batch of homemade cookies in our bag. These cookies pair the classic combination of chocolate and walnuts, but with the unexpected addition of tahini and *fleur de sel,* they are even easier to fall for.

Preheat the oven to 375°F (190°C). Line 2 baking sheets with parchment paper; set aside.

In the bowl of a stand mixer, beat the butter, sugar, and tahini until the texture is creamy. Beat in the vanilla and egg. If necessary, scrape the sides of the bowl a few times while beating.

In a separate bowl, combine the flours, quinoa flakes, *fleur de sel,* and baking soda. Add to the butter mixture, stirring just until the ingredients are incorporated. Using a spatula, stir in the chocolate and nuts.

Drop heaping tablespoons of batter onto the baking sheets, making sure to leave 2-inch spaces between the cookies, as they spread slightly while cooking. Place in the oven and bake for 14 minutes, or until golden in color. Remove from the oven and, using a spatula, transfer immediately to a cooling rack.

When I bake cookies, I prefer to bake one batch at a time, to make sure the heat is uniform. Experiment for yourself and see what works best for you.

Makes sixteen 3-inch cookies

6 tablespoons (80 g; 2 ¾ oz) unsalted butter, softened

⅔ cup (100 g; 3 ½ oz) light Muscovado sugar

2 tablespoons tahini (sesame butter)

1 teaspoon pure vanilla extract

1 large egg

½ cup (60 g; 2 oz) millet flour

¼ cup (45 g; 1 ½ oz) brown rice flour

¼ cup (30 g; 1 oz) quinoa flour

½ cup (60 g; 2 oz) quinoa flakes

¼ teaspoon *fleur de sel*

½ teaspoon baking soda

¾ cup (100 g; 3 ½ oz) dark chocolate (70% cocoa), coarsely chopped

3 oz (90 g) walnuts, coarsely chopped

White chocolate, oat, and cranberries cookies
with fleur de sel

Makes sixteen to eighteen 3-inch cookies

½ cup (60 g; 2 oz) quinoa flour

¼ cup (30 g; 1 oz) millet flour

¼ cup (45 g; 1 ½ oz) brown rice flour

½ cup (50 g; 1 ¾ oz) rolled oats or quinoa flakes

½ teaspoon baking soda

¼ teaspoon *fleur de sel*

8 tablespoons (113 g; 4 oz) unsalted butter, softened

⅔ packed cup (110 g; 3 ¾ oz) light brown sugar

1 small egg

1 teaspoon pure vanilla extract

¾ cup (100 g; 3 ½ oz) slivered almonds or coarsely chopped walnuts

¾ cup (125 g; 4 ½ oz) coarsely chopped white chocolate

½ cup (60 g; 2 oz) dried cranberries

These cookies are wholesome and light with just the right amount of sweet. You'll love the refreshing zesty flavor the cranberries bring.

Preheat the oven to 375°F (190°C). Line 2 baking sheets with parchment paper; set aside.

In a bowl, combine the flours, the rolled oats, baking soda, and *fleur de sel*; set aside.

In the bowl of a stand mixer, beat the butter with the sugar until light and pale in color. Stir in the egg until well incorporated, then add the vanilla and the flour mixture; mix until just incorporated. Fold in the nuts, white chocolate, and cranberries.

Drop heaping tablespoons of batter onto the baking sheets, making sure to leave 2-inch spaces between the cookies, as they spread slightly while cooking. Place in the oven and bake for 14 minutes, or until the cookies are light golden in color. Remove from the oven and, using a spatula, transfer immediately to a cooling rack. The cookies will firm up while cooling. Keep them in an airtight container for up to 1 week.

I like cranberries because of their tanginess and cheery bright color, even once dried, but feel free to replace them with other dried fruits, such as cherries or raisins.

BEAUTIFUL AND IRRESISTIBLE DESSERTS

When I was younger and a lover of anything involving sugar, my mother took notice and used it to her advantage. Since she didn't care much for preparing elaborate desserts herself, whenever guests were invited for dinner, she'd asked that I prepare dessert. She was smart. She *liked* that I was fond of making dessert, and I was proud that I was good at it.

All along, though, I could never settle on just one dessert. So I always made two, just in case the first one didn't turn out right or the guests might dislike a specific ingredient. I haven't let go of this habit, so when friends come over, the chance of two desserts on the table is fairly high. It gives me a great excuse to practice, and I sense that no one minds.

I find making beautiful, elaborate desserts challenging . . . but so rewarding! Take cakes, for example. While the average cake that I bake is rustic, when we have a special dinner or an occasion to celebrate, I want to dress it up so it's pretty and irresistible. So I'll make a dessert that will elicit *oohs* and *aahs* when it's revealed.

That special cake will often offer different flavors and layers of textures. Sometimes dark and white chocolate mousses are enclosed between slices of a light sponge cake. Other times

I'll fill a *charlotte* with a fruit mousse and fresh slices of fruit. Or maybe it will be a sweet tart with a lot of character—like a tangy and sweet Meyer lemon tart. Have you ever tried one before?

It's easy to become addicted to making elegant-looking desserts once you get the hang of it. Preparing those desserts feels like drawing or painting a beautiful canvas, only in this case, the imagination flows freely to create sweets that are colorful and tasty. It makes you feel proud to say *"C'est moi qui l'ai fait!"* ("I made it!") when your guests inquire, wide-eyed, about what you've brought to the table. It makes me feel happy and know it was well worth the effort. And inevitably, I'm inspired to rush back into the kitchen to experiment with a new dessert idea for the next time.

Strawberry and raspberry charlotte

I remember summers when my mother would prepare a *charlotte* with juicy and plump berries. She always made it on Sundays or for special occasions. This made me impatient for guests to come for dinner as often as possible. And I still find *charlottes* irresistible—the quintessence of a light dessert that you can eat a few helpings of without even noticing. It's a wonderful eye-catching dessert that requires a few steps, especially because rather than buying ladyfingers to use in the dessert, I prefer to bake them myself, but it's completely worth the extra effort.

Notes: The charlotte *can be prepared a day in advance of serving it. Also, feel free to substitute another type of berry for the strawberries, if you prefer.*

Makes one 7-inch charlotte*; serves 6*

You will need: an 8-inch springform pan and an adjustable cake ring mold

For the strawberry syrup:
2 oz (60 g) strawberries (about 2 medium strawberries), hulled
5 tablespoons water
¼ cup (50 g; 1 ¾ oz) blond cane sugar
1 tablespoon lemon or lime juice

For the raspberry sauce:
10 ½ oz (300 g) raspberries
4 tablespoons confectioners' sugar
Dash of lemon or lime juice

For the sponge cake:
Unsalted butter, for the mold
2 large eggs, separated
¼ cup plus 1 tablespoon (60 g; 2 oz) blond cane sugar
1 ½ tablespoons (22 g; ¾ oz) unsalted butter, melted and cooled
1 teaspoon pure vanilla extract
3 tablespoons quinoa flour
2 tablespoons white rice flour
1 tablespoon strawberry syrup (see above)
Pinch of sea salt

For the strawberry mousse:
14 oz (400 g) strawberries, hulled
⅓ cup plus 1 tablespoon (85 g; 3 oz) blond cane sugar
1 tablespoon lemon or lime juice
4 gelatin sheets (8 g; .2 oz), or 2 teaspoons gelatin powder
2 large egg whites
Pinch of sea salt
⅔ cup (160 ml) cold heavy cream

About 15 ladyfingers (see Basic Recipes, page 24)
7 oz (200 g) raspberries for the filling, plus 3 ½ oz (100 g), to decorate
3 oz (90 g) strawberries, hulled and sliced, to decorate

To prepare the strawberry syrup: Using a food processor, purée the strawberries. Transfer the strawberry pulp to a *chinois* or fine sieve and strain to remove the seeds, pressing down on the fruit to extract all the juice. In a small pot, heat the water with the sugar over medium heat and stir until the sugar is dissolved; remove from the heat and let cool. Stir in the strawberry purée and lemon juice; set aside.

To prepare the raspberry sauce: Using a food processor, purée the raspberries with the confectioners' sugar. Transfer the raspberry pulp to a *chinois* or a fine sieve and strain to remove the seeds, pressing down on the fruit to extract all the juice. Stir in the lemon juice and refrigerate until ready to serve.

To prepare the sponge cake: Preheat the oven to 350°F (180°C). Butter the springform pan and cut a piece of parchment paper to cover the bottom; set aside.

In the bowl of a stand mixer, beat the egg yolks with ¼ cup of the sugar until light and pale in color. Stir in the melted butter, vanilla, and flours. Add the strawberry syrup and mix well.

In a separate bowl, beat the egg whites with the sea salt until soft peaks form. Add the remaining 1 tablespoon sugar and continue to beat for 1 minute. Stir 1 tablespoon of the egg whites into the cake batter, then gently fold in the rest of the egg whites, making sure to keep the batter light.

Pour the batter into the cake pan and bake for 12 to 15 minutes, until it feels springy to the touch. Remove from the oven and unmold onto a rack; let cool.

To prepare the strawberry mousse: Using a food processor, purée the strawberries with ⅓ cup of the sugar and the lemon juice; set aside. Soak the gelatin sheets in a large bowl of cold water for 5 to 10 minutes. Using your fingertips, squeeze the excess water out of the gelatin. In a pot, heat 2 tablespoons of the strawberry purée; when warm, remove from the heat and add the gelatin sheets, stirring continuously until they are dissolved. Stir in the rest of the strawberry purée.

In a bowl, beat the egg whites with the sea salt until soft peaks form. Add the remaining 1 tablespoon sugar and continue to beat for 1 minute. Fold the egg whites into the strawberry purée. In a separate bowl, beat the heavy cream with an electric mixer until it forms soft peaks. Fold it gently into the strawberry purée mixture; set aside.

To assemble the charlotte: Cut the sponge cake into a 6 ½-inch circle and place it at the bottom of your ring mold. Make sure the ring mold is secure. Arrange the ladyfingers vertically along the sides of the mold with the sugared side facing out. Brush the cake and ladyfingers with strawberry syrup. Arrange the raspberries on top of the sponge cake and cover with the strawberry mousse, using a spatula to make the mousse even. Cover the charlotte with plastic wrap and refrigerate for about 4 hours or overnight. Remove the ring mold and decorate with raspberries and sliced strawberries. Serve on dessert plates and drizzle with the raspberry sauce.

Cardamom-flavored chocolate crème caramel

Serves 6

You will need: six 6-ounce ramekins

Canola oil, for the ramekins

For the caramel:
½ cup (100 g: 3 ½ oz) fine granulated
    white sugar
2 tablespoons cold water
1 tablespoon hot water

For the chocolate custard:
2 ¼ cups (530 ml) whole milk
1 vanilla bean, split open and seeds
    scraped out
5 green cardamom pods, crushed
3 oz (90 g) dark chocolate
    (70% cocoa)
3 large eggs
2 tablespoons blond cane sugar
Unsweetened cocoa powder,
    to dust

This attractive dessert is made for people like me and Philip who cannot resist anything described with words like "dark chocolate" and "custard." Maybe you are one of these people too? It offers a rich silky aromatic chocolate flanlike cream balanced by a light caramel sauce that you'll want to dip your fingers into.

Oil six 6-ounce ramekins; set aside.

To prepare the caramel: Heat the sugar and cold water in a small pot. Swirl the pot in a circular movement so that the sugar absorbs the water. Bring to a boil, then simmer at a medium heat—do not stir the sugar at this point, although you can swirl the pot occasionally—and watch the caramel develop. It will be ready when it's golden in color, which takes about 8 to 10 minutes. Remove from the heat, add the hot water, and stir quickly. Pour the caramel into the oiled ramekins, making sure to coat the bottom and sides; set aside.

Preheat the oven to 300°F (150°C).

To prepare the custard: In a pot, combine the milk with the vanilla bean and seeds and cardamom pods and bring to a boil, making sure that it doesn't overflow. When it boils, remove from the heat and add the chocolate, whisking quickly so that the chocolate melts evenly. Cover and let infuse for 20 minutes. Discard the vanilla bean and cardamom, and using a fine sieve or *chinois*, strain the chocolate milk.

In the meantime, using a stand mixer, beat the eggs with the sugar for 1 minute. Pour the chocolate milk in and stir quickly. With a spoon, remove any foam that might have formed at the surface.

Divide the chocolate custard among the 6 caramel-filled ramekins and place them in a water bath (see Basic Cooking Techniques, page 27, for instructions). Place the custards in the oven and cook for about 50 minutes. To check if they are ready, jiggle the ramekins a little—the center of the cream should be almost set but not fully (they'll finish setting once they cool down). Remove the ramekins from the oven and let cool completely. Cover each ramekin with plastic wrap and refrigerate for a few hours, or overnight, until the custard is completely set.

To unmold the *crème caramel* easily, dip the ramekins in boiling water for 1 to 2 minutes, taking care to not let the water spill in. Run the blade of a knife between the custard and the edge of the ramekins. Turn onto a plate and serve with dusted cocoa on top.

Apple and pear verrines

with millet crumble and vanilla custard

The day I made these *verrines*, I was in the mood for an apple tart with warm custard, *papa*'s (Philip's late grandfather) favorite dessert, but I didn't have a crust ready. So came the idea of recomposing the dessert inside a glass. I used leftovers of a crumble topping made for another dessert and delicious Macoun apples and Forelle pears bought at the farmers' market. The rest followed naturally to make a beautiful dessert that *papa* would have had a weakness for too, just as Philip did. The custard gene runs deep in the family.

Makes 6 verrines

For the stewed apples and pears:

2 apples, peeled, cored, and diced (choose sweet baking apples)

2 ripe pears (Forelle or Bosc), peeled, cored, and diced

Finely grated zest of ½ organic lemon

1 cinnamon stick

½ vanilla bean, split open and seeds scraped out

¼ cup (50 g; 1 ¾ oz) blond cane sugar

¼ cup (60 ml) cold water

Juice of ½ lemon

For the vanilla-flavored *crème anglaise*:

1 ½ cups (350 ml) whole milk

1 vanilla bean, split open and seeds scraped out

5 large egg yolks

3 tablespoons blond cane sugar

2 teaspoons cornstarch

For the millet crumble:

3 tablespoons millet flour

3 tablespoons quinoa flakes

3 tablespoons almond meal

¾ oz (20 g) chopped walnuts

½ oz (15 g) shelled unsalted green pistachios, chopped

3 tablespoons light Muscovado sugar

½ teaspoon pure vanilla extract

2 ½ tablespoons (35 g; 1 ¼ oz) unsalted butter, chilled

For the sautéed apple:

1 tablespoon (14 g; ½ oz) unsalted butter

1 large tangy and sweet apple (such as pink lady), peeled, cored, and diced

1 tablespoon blond cane sugar

Lemon juice, to drizzle

To prepare the stewed fruit: In a pot, combine the apples, pears, lemon zest, cinnamon stick, vanilla bean and seeds, sugar, and water. Bring to a boil, then reduce the heat and simmer for 20 minutes, or until the fruit is soft. Discard the vanilla bean and cinnamon stick and purée the fruit. Add the lemon juice; set aside.

To prepare the *crème anglaise*: In a pot, combine the milk with the vanilla bean and seeds and bring to a boil over medium heat, making sure that it doesn't overflow. When it reaches the boiling point, remove from the heat, cover, and leave to infuse for 15 minutes. Using a fine sieve or *chinois*, strain the milk to remove any skin that might have formed at the surface. Return the milk to the pot with the vanilla bean and cover to keep warm.

Meanwhile, in a bowl, beat the egg yolks with the sugar until light and pale in color. Add the cornstarch and mix well. Pour the milk in slowly, stirring constantly. Transfer the mixture back to the pot and cook over medium-low heat, stirring constantly, until the cream thickens—it should never boil. The custard is ready when it coats a spoon—this takes between 5 and 6 minutes. Once the cream is ready, remove the vanilla bean and transfer to a bowl. Let cool, stirring occasionally; set aside.

To prepare the crumble: Preheat the oven to 350°F (180°C). Cover a baking sheet with parchment paper; set aside.

In a bowl, combine the millet flour, quinoa flakes, almond meal, walnuts, pistachios, sugar, and vanilla. Add the butter and work with your fingertips until crumbles form. Spread the crumble uniformly over the baking sheet and bake for about 15 minutes, until lightly browned. Stir occasionally with a spoon while it's baking so that it cooks evenly. Remove from the oven and let cool completely at room temperature.

To prepare the sautéed apple: In a frying pan, melt the butter. Add the apple and sugar and cook for 2 to 3 minutes, stirring. Transfer to a small bowl and drizzle with lemon juice; set aside.

To assemble the *verrines*: Divide the stewed fruit among 6 dessert glasses. Layer with the sautéed apples. Pour the vanilla custard over the fruit, finish with the millet crumble, and serve.

Dark and white chocolate mousse cake

When our friend Ron invited us for Thanksgiving dinner, he asked that I bring dessert.

"Qu'est-ce que tu crois que je peux faire?" ("What do you think I should make?") I had asked Philip. "Whatever you think will look amazing!" So I made this two-chocolate mousse cake. I knew it wasn't a conventional Thanksgiving dessert, and thought perhaps I should have baked a pecan or pumpkin pie. But when Ron's mother, Irene, ninety-six years of age at the time, asked for a third helping and kept repeating, "It's really good!" with her mouth still full, I knew it was the right dessert to bring. And now, whenever I make this cake, I smile thinking about her.

Makes one 8-inch round cake or four individual cakes

You will need: a 9-inch springform mold and an 8-inch ring mold (or 2 ¾-inch-wide by 2 ¼-inch-tall ring molds for individual cakes)

For the chocolate cake:

1 ½ tablespoons (22 g; ¾ oz) unsalted butter, plus more for the mold

Flour of your choice, to dust the mold

2 ½ oz (70 g) dark chocolate (70 % cocoa)

3 large eggs, separated

2 tablespoons light Muscovado sugar

1 tablespoon blond cane sugar

½ teaspoon pure vanilla extract

Pinch of sea salt

1 tablespoon cornstarch, sifted

10 ½ oz (300 g) fresh raspberries (optional)

For the hazelnut chocolate mousse:

1 gelatin sheet (2 g; .07 oz), or ½ teaspoon gelatin powder

2 ½ oz (75 g) dark chocolate (64% cocoa)

1 ¾ oz (50 g) hazelnut-flavored chocolate

¼ cup (60 ml) whole milk

¾ cup (180 ml) cold heavy cream

For the white chocolate mousse:

¼ cup (60 ml) whole milk

6 green cardamom pods, crushed

1 vanilla bean, split open and seeds scraped out

1 gelatin sheet (2 g; .07 oz), or ½ teaspoon gelatin powder

4 ½ oz (125 g) white chocolate

¾ cup (180 ml) cold heavy cream

Unsweetened cocoa powder, to dust and serve

Shaved white chocolate, to serve

Shaved dark chocolate, to serve

To prepare the chocolate cake: Preheat the oven to 350°F (180°C). Cut a circle of parchment paper to the size of the bottom of your 9-inch springform mold. Butter the mold (bottom and sides) and line the bottom with the paper. Flour the sides and tap the excess off.

Melt the chocolate and 1 ½ tablespoons butter in a bain-marie (see Basic Cooking Techniques, page 27; set aside.

In the bowl of a stand mixer, beat the egg yolks with the two sugars until light and pale in color. Stir in the vanilla and then the melted chocolate and butter mixture. In a separate bowl, beat the egg whites with a pinch of sea salt until soft peaks form. Gently fold the egg whites into the cake batter a third at a time, making sure to keep the batter light. Add the cornstarch and fold gently again.

Pour the batter into the cake mold, place in the oven, and bake for about 12 minutes, until the top of the cake feels springy. Remove from the oven and let cool slightly, then unmold on a cooling rack and carefully remove the parchment paper.

Cut the base of the cake to fit the size of your ring mold. Line the ring mold with a plastic cake wrap and place the cake at the bottom of the mold. If using, arrange the raspberries on top of the chocolate cake base and set aside.

To prepare the hazelnut chocolate mousse: Soak the gelatin sheet in large bowl of cold water for 5 to 10 minutes. Using your fingertips, squeeze out the excess water from the gelatin sheets. Melt the chocolates in a bain-marie (see Basic Cooking Techniques, page 27, for instructions); transfer to a large bowl and set aside. Heat the milk until it feels hot to the touch. Remove from heat and add the gelatin sheets, stirring continuously until they are dissolved. Pour the milk into the chocolate a little bit at a time, stirring constantly and quickly with a rubber spatula; let the mixture sit for 5 minutes. Beat the heavy cream with an electric mixer until it forms soft peaks and fold it gently into the chocolate batter.

Pour the hazelnut chocolate mousse on top of the chocolate cake and level it with spatula. Refrigerate the cake while you prepare the white chocolate mousse.

To prepare the white chocolate mousse: In a pot, heat the milk with the cardamom and vanilla bean and seeds. Remove from the heat, cover, and leave to infuse for 30 minutes. Using a fine sieve or *chinois,* strain the milk.

In the meantime, soak the gelatin sheet in large bowl of cold water for 5 to 10 minutes. Using your fingertips, squeeze out the excess water from the gelatin sheets. Melt the chocolate in a bain-marie; transfer to a large bowl and set aside. Heat the milk again until it feels hot to the touch. Remove from heat and add the gelatin sheets, stirring continuously until they are dissolved. Pour the milk into the chocolate a little bit at a time, stirring constantly and quickly with a rubber spatula; let the mixture sit for 5 minutes. Whip the heavy cream with an electric mixer until it forms soft peaks and fold it gently into the white chocolate batter.

Pour the white chocolate mousse on top of the dark chocolate mousse and refrigerate for 3 hours, or until the chocolate mousses are set, or overnight if you're preparing the cakes the day before serving.

To serve, dust with cocoa powder and top with shaved white and dark chocolate. Transfer the cake onto a serving dish and carefully remove the ring mold and cake wrap. Et voilà!

Tip: When I prepare the cake, I like to place it on a plate covered with a piece of parchment paper. This makes it easier to transfer the cake to the serving plate. Also, if you prefer to prepare individual cakes, you will have sponge cake leftovers, which is just delicious to nibble on.

Meyer lemon tart

My father drinks freshly squeezed lemon juice every morning. No sugar. That's more than I can do; yet I am a real lemon lover — and would go to great lengths for the taste of a lemon tart. Lemon must be running in our genes, after all.

This tart has a cream that will make you lick your fingers. I make it with Meyer lemons — my favorite lemons for their milder and sweeter taste — but limes, regular lemons, or even clementines, would be delicious too.

Makes one 9-inch tart

You will need: a 9-inch tart mold

Pâte sucrée (see Basic Recipes, page 21) flavored with lemon zest (add the finely grated zest of 1 lemon to the dry ingredients when you are preparing the crust)

For the raspberry sauce:
7 oz (200 g) raspberries
2 tablespoons blond cane sugar
½ teaspoon cornstarch

For the lemon cream:
3 large eggs plus 1 large egg yolk
⅔ cup (80 g; 2 ¾ oz) blond cane sugar
Juice of 4 Meyer lemons, plus the finely grated zest of 1 (makes between ⅔ cup to ¾ cup of juice)
6 tablespoons (90 g; 3 oz) unsalted butter, chilled and diced

To prepare the raspberry sauce: Using a food processor, purée the raspberries with the sugar. Transfer the raspberry purée to a *chinois* or fine sieve to remove the seeds. Transfer the pulp to a pot and bring to a simmer. Stir in the cornstarch and cook for 1 minute. Remove from the heat and let cool.

To prepare the lemon cream: In a bowl, beat the eggs, egg yolk, sugar, and lemon zest and juice to combine. Transfer the mixture to a pot and add the butter. Warm over low heat until the butter melts, stirring constantly. Continue stirring until the cream thickens, making sure it doesn't boil. The cream is ready when it becomes denser and coats a spoon well.

To prepare the tart: Preheat the oven to 350°F (180°C). Roll the dough and garnish your mold with it. Using a fork, make small holes at the bottom of the crust. Refrigerate for 30 minutes, then prebake for 15 minutes (see Basic Cooking Techniques, page 27, for instructions). Remove the parchment paper and weights, and brush the bottom of the crust with the egg white. Bake again for 5 minutes. Remove from the oven and let cool slightly.

Pour the lemon cream into the crust and drizzle with the raspberry sauce. Using a fork, drag the raspberry sauce to create a pattern on the surface of the tart. Return the tart to the oven and bake it again for 15 minutes. Remove from the oven and let cool completely before serving.

Tonka bean—flavored chocolate mousse and vanilla custard cakes

The story of how these delicious multilayered cakes ended up in my kitchen is one that I will never forget. I tested my recipe for the first time a week before Christmas, with the intention of baking and serving the cakes again on Christmas day. I remember how excited I was about the outcome and how pretty the contrast of colors from the different layers looked once arranged together. But life took the lead, eventually changing my plan—instead of cakes, it gave us Lulu, our beautiful baby daughter, born in the early morning on Christmas day. So perhaps the cakes never made it to Christmas, but they gave me a wonderful story that one day I will share with Lulu.

These cakes have four different layers of goodness: a dark chocolate sponge cake, a dark and milk chocolate mousse, a vanilla-flavored pastry cream, and a tonka bean sponge cake. Yes, they require more work than what you and I might make on a daily basis, but they're a gorgeous dressed-up dessert to make for a special occasion.

Makes 6 individual cakes

You will need: six 2 ¾-inch-wide by 2 ¼-inch-tall ring molds with plastic cake wraps to place inside; and one 9-inch springform mold

For the chocolate cake:
1 ½ tablespoons (22 g; ¾ oz) unsalted butter, plus more for the mold
Flour of your choice, to dust the mold
2 ½ oz (70 g) dark chocolate (70% cocoa)
3 large eggs, separated
2 tablespoons light Muscovado sugar
1 tablespoon blond cane sugar
½ teaspoon pure vanilla extract
Pinch of sea salt
1 tablespoon cornstarch, sifted

For the tonka bean sponge cake:
Unsalted butter, for the mold
2 large eggs
¼ cup (50 g; 1 ¾ oz) blond cane sugar
Pinch of sea salt
½ tonka bean, finely grated (use a nutmeg grater), or 1 teaspoon pure vanilla extract
1 tablespoon (14 g; ½ oz) unsalted butter, melted
3 tablespoons brown rice flour
3 tablespoons quinoa flour

For the dark and milk chocolate mousse:
2 oz (60 g) dark chocolate (64% cocoa)
2 oz (60 g) milk chocolate (40% cocoa)
1 gelatin sheet (2 g; .07 oz), or ½ teaspoon gelatin powder

¼ cup (60 ml) whole milk
¾ cup (180 ml) cold heavy cream

For the vanilla custard:
1 ½ cups (350 ml) whole milk
1 vanilla bean, split open and seeds scraped out
3 large egg yolks
¼ cup (50 g; 1 ¾ oz) blond cane sugar
3 tablespoons (30 g; 1 oz) cornstarch
1 ½ tablespoons unsalted butter, diced
Unsweetened cocoa powder, to serve
Confectioners' sugar, to serve
240 g (8 ½ oz) mixed crystallized berries, or mixed fresh berries, to serve

To prepare the chocolate cake: Preheat the oven to 350°F (180°C). Cut a circle of parchment paper to the size of the bottom of your 9-inch springform mold. Butter the mold (bottom and sides) and line the bottom with the paper. Flour the sides and tap the excess off.

Melt the chocolate and butter in a bain-marie (see Basic Cooking Techniques, page 27, for instructions); set aside.

In the bowl of a stand mixer, beat the egg yolks with the two sugars until light and pale in color. Stir in the vanilla and then the melted chocolate and butter mixture. In a separate bowl, beat the egg whites with a pinch of sea salt until soft peaks form. Gently fold the egg whites into the cake batter a third at a time, making sure to keep the batter light. Add the cornstarch and gently fold again. Pour the batter into the cake mold and bake for about 12 minutes, until the top of the cake feels springy. Remove from the oven and let cool for 5 minutes before unmolding. Remove the parchment paper carefully and let cool completely on a cooling rack.

Cut 6 circles out of the cake to the size of the ring molds; you should have exactly enough for 6. Line the ring molds with the plastic cake wrap and place the circles of cake at the bottom of the molds; set aside.

To prepare the tonka bean sponge cake: Preheat the oven to 350°F (180°C). Butter the 9-inch springform mold. Cut a circle of parchment paper to the size of the mold and place the circle in the bottom of the mold.

Place a bowl over a pot of simmering water, making sure that the bottom of the bowl does not touch the water. Break the eggs into the bowl and add the sugar and salt. Using an electric hand mixer, beat the eggs with the sugar until light and pale in color and the egg mixture is warm to the touch and forms soft peaks; this takes about 4 minutes. Remove from heat and continue to beat for 2 to 3 minutes. Stir in the tonka bean and melted butter. Sprinkle the flours on top and fold in gently, making sure to keep the batter light. Pour the batter into the mold so that it spreads evenly, place in the oven, and bake for 12 minutes, or until the top feels springy to the touch. Remove from the oven and let cool for 5 minutes before unmolding. Remove the parchment paper carefully and let cool completely on a cooling rack. Cut 6 circles out of the cake to the size of the ring molds—again, you should have exactly enough for 6; set aside.

Tonka bean is fragrant spice — a cross between almond and vanilla, with hints of cinnamon and cloves — that you can use as you would vanilla to flavor custards and cakes. It's mainly produced in Venezuela and Nigeria, and it's interesting to know that the spice is actually banned in the United States due to its coumarin content, a substance that can be lethal if eaten in large doses (just like nutmeg). However, the bean is largely used everywhere else, including in France, where it is currently a fashionable ingredient in many upscale restaurants. Naturally, it piqued my curiosity. If you prefer not to use tonka bean, substitute vanilla, as suggested in the recipe that follows.

To prepare the dark and milk chocolate mousse: Melt the two chocolates in a bain-marie; transfer to a larger bowl. In the meantime, soak the gelatin sheet in a bowl of cold water for 5 minutes. Using your fingertips, squeeze out the excess water. Heat the milk until it feels hot to the touch. Remove from heat and add the gelatin sheet, stirring continuously until dissolved. Pour the milk into the chocolate a little bit at a time, stirring constantly with a rubber spatula; let the mixture sit for 5 minutes. Beat the heavy cream with an electric mixer until it forms soft peaks and gently fold it into the chocolate. Transfer the mousse to a pastry bag and pipe it among the 6 ring molds, spreading it over the chocolate sponge cake (if you do not have a pastry bag, spoon the mousse evenly over the sponge cake). Refrigerate while you prepare the next step.

To prepare the vanilla custard: In a pot, heat the milk with the vanilla bean and seeds. When it reaches the boiling pot, remove from the heat; cover and leave to infuse for 30 minutes. Using a fine sieve or *chinois,* strain the milk and warm again. In the meantime, in the bowl of a stand mixer, beat the egg yolks with the sugar until light and pale in color. Reduce the speed of your mixer and beat the cornstarch in. Continue to beat while you slowly pour the milk in. Transfer the custard back to the pot and cook over medium heat, stirring constantly, until the custard reaches the first boiling point and it becomes thicker in texture—a bubble will form at the surface of the custard, showing that the right temperature is reached. Remove from the heat and transfer the custard to a bowl. Place the bowl in an ice-water bath to allow the custard to cool and stir in the butter. Stir the custard occasionally to prevent a crust from forming at the surface. When completely cooled, cover the custard with plastic wrap and refrigerate until ready to use.

To assemble the cakes: Pour the custard evenly among the 6 ring molds, spreading it on top of the chocolate mousse. Finish assembling the cake by adding the final layer of tonka bean sponge cake. Refrigerate the cakes for a few hours, or overnight. When you are ready to serve, transfer the cakes onto serving plates. Carefully remove the ring molds and cake wraps. Dust the cakes with cocoa and confectioners' sugar and decorate with crystallized or fresh berries.

> *To make crystallized berries, lightly beat an egg white and dip the berries in it. Sprinkle the berries lightly with fine granulated white sugar so that the sugar coats them and let them dry on a cooling rack at room temperature for 1 hour minimum, or even overnight.*

Rhubarb mousse fraisier

A *fraisier* (a strawberry cake) is supposed to celebrate the arrival of the first strawberries and it does so wonderfully—the cake is a star in French *pâtisseries* in spring. It's traditionally made of a light two-layer sponge cake (*une génoise*) filled with *crème mousseline* (a combination of pasty cream and butter cream) and fresh, juicy strawberries, and is then covered with a thin sheet of almond paste. In my version of this delicious dessert, I prefer to make individual cakes, and I use a light rhubarb mousse and leave the almond paste out too. These treats are so light and delicate that, after eating one, you may wonder if it was only a dream that you just consumed a cake!

Makes 4 individual cakes

You will need: four 2 ¾-inch-wide by 2 ¼-inch-tall ring molds with plastic cake wraps to place inside; and a 9-inch springform mold

For the vanilla sponge cake:
Unsalted butter, for the mold
2 large eggs
¼ cup (50 g; 1 ¾ oz) blond cane sugar, plus 1 tablespoon for the egg whites
Pinch of sea salt
1 teaspoon pure vanilla extract
1 tablespoon (14 g; ½ oz) unsalted butter, melted

3 tablespoons quinoa flour, sifted
3 tablespoons white or brown rice flour

For the strawberry syrup:
4 medium strawberries
3 tablespoons (40 g; 1 ½ oz) blond cane sugar
5 tablespoons water
1 tablespoon lemon juice

For the rhubarb mousse:
9 oz (250 g) rhubarb, peeled and diced (makes 2 cups once cleaned and cut into 1-inch pieces)
¼ cup (50 g; 1 ¾ oz) blond cane sugar

2 tablespoons cold water
1 tablespoon lemon juice
2 gelatin sheets (4 g; .14 oz), or 1 teaspoon gelatin powder
½ cup (120 ml) cold heavy cream
4 ½ oz (125 g) *mascarpone* cheese
¼ cup (30 g; 1 oz) confectioners' sugar, sifted
½ vanilla bean, split open and seeds scraped out
2 small egg whites
Pinch of sea salt

1 pound 2 oz (500 g) strawberries, preferably small to medium, hulled, cut in half, and sliced
Mint leaves, to decorate
Confectioners' sugar, to serve

To prepare the vanilla sponge cake: Preheat the oven to 350°F (180°C). Butter the 9-inch springform mold. Cut a circle of parchment paper of the size of the mold and place the circle in the bottom of the mold.

Place a bowl over a pot of simmering water, making sure that the bottom of the bowl does not touch the water. Break the eggs into the bowl and add the sugar and sea salt. Using an electric hand mixer, beat the eggs and sugar until light and pale in color, and the egg mixture is warm to the touch and forms soft peaks; this takes about 4 minutes. Remove from the heat and continue to beat for 2 to 3 more minutes. Stir in the vanilla and melted butter. Sprinkle the flours on top and fold in gently, making sure to keep the batter light. Pour the batter into the mold so that it spreads evenly, place in the oven, and bake for 12 minutes, or until the top feels springy to the touch. Remove from the oven and let cool slightly before unmolding. Remove the parchment paper carefully and let cool completely on a cooling rack. Cut 6 circles out of the cake to the size of the ring molds. Place the plastic cake wraps inside each mold and add a circle of cake at the bottom of each one; set aside.

To prepare the strawberry syrup: In a pot, combine the sugar with the water and boil for 1 minute. Using a food processor, purée the strawberries with the syrup. Transfer to a fine sieve or *chinois* and strain to remove the seeds. Stir in the lemon juice and strawberry pulp; set aside.

To prepare the rhubarb mousse: In a pot, combine the rhubarb with the sugar and water. Cook over medium-low heat until the rhubarb softens; this takes about 5 minutes. Add the lemon juice to the rhubarb and purée; let cool and set aside.

Soak the gelatin sheets in a large bowl of cold water for 5 to 10 minutes. Using the tips of your fingers, squeeze the gelatin to remove the excess water. In a pot, heat 2 tablespoons of the heavy cream. When hot, remove from the heat and add the gelatin sheets, stirring until they dissolve.

In a bowl, beat the *mascarpone* with the confectioners' sugar and vanilla seeds with a whisk until smooth. Stir in the rhubarb purée. In a separate bowl, beat the egg whites with a pinch of sea salt until they form soft peaks. Fold the egg whites into the rhubarb mousse. In another bowl, beat the rest of the heavy cream with an electric mixer until it forms soft peaks. Gently fold the cream into the mousse; set aside.

To assemble the cake: Brush each sponge cake with strawberry syrup. Arrange the strawberry halves on the cake bases with the cut face placed against the liner and the pointy end up. Fill the middles now with more strawberries arranged in the same way. Transfer the rhubarb mousse to a pastry bag and pipe it on top (if you do not have a pastry bag, spoon the mousse evenly over the sponge cake). Use a knife or flat spatula to level the mousse. Cover the cakes with plastic wrap and refrigerate for a few hours or overnight, until the mousse is set. When you are ready to serve, transfer the cakes onto serving plates. Carefully remove the ring molds and cake wraps. Decorate with a few strawberry slices and mint leaves and dust with confectioners' sugar.

Raspberry tiramisu in a glass

Makes 4 glasses

For the almond crumble topping:

3 tablespoons almond meal

3 tablespoons quinoa flour

3 tablespoons quinoa flakes

3 tablespoons packed light Muscovado sugar

1 vanilla bean, split open and seeds
   scraped out

¾ oz (20 g) walnuts, coarsely chopped

½ oz (15 g) shelled unsalted green
   pistachios, coarsely chopped

2 ½ tablespoons (35 g; 1 ¼ oz)
   unsalted butter, chilled and diced

For the raspberry sauce:

12 oz (340 g) raspberries

3 tablespoons blond cane sugar

1 teaspoon cornstarch

1 teaspoon lime juice

For the *mascarpone* cream:

9 oz (255 g) *mascarpone* cheese

2 extra-fresh large eggs, separated

4 tablespoons blond cane sugar

1 teaspoon pure vanilla extract

Pinch of sea salt

16 homemade ladyfingers (see Basic
   Recipes, page 24), coarsely
   crumbled

Confectioners' sugar, to dust

½ oz (15 g) shelled unsalted green
   pistachios, finely chopped

2 oz (60 g) raspberries, to decorate

> "Is there more?" Philip asked anxiously after swallowing a spoonful of the *tiramisu* I handed to him. I felt exactly the same way. You'll see—besides looking colorful and pretty when served individually in a small glass, this raspberry tiramisu feels light, urging you for more.
>
> *"Cela passe comme une lettre à la poste, n'est-ce pas?"* ("It goes down like a letter in the mailbox, doesn't it?") I added with my mouth full. We smiled at each other silently, and then dipped our spoons into our glasses for more.

To prepare the almond crumble topping: Preheat the oven to 350°F (180°C). Cover a baking sheet with parchment paper; set aside.

In a bowl, combine the almond meal with the quinoa flour, quinoa flakes, and sugar. Mix in the vanilla seeds and nuts. Add the butter and work with your fingertips until coarse crumbles form. Transfer the crumbles to the baking sheet; spread evenly.

Place in the oven and bake for 12 to 15 minutes, until lightly browned, tossing regularly with a spoon and checking that it doesn't burn. Remove from the oven, let cool, and set aside. If you make this the night before, you can store it in the fridge in a plastic bag or airtight container; bring back to room temperature before using.

To prepare the raspberry sauce: In a small pot, heat 7 oz of the raspberries with the sugar. Bring to a simmer and using a fork, mash the raspberries while the fruit is softening. Stir in the cornstarch and simmer for 1 minute, or until the sauce thickens slightly. Remove from the heat and stir in the lime juice; set aside to cool. Once cooled, fold the rest of the raspberries into the sauce; set aside.

To prepare the *mascarpone* cream: In a large bowl, use a whisk to beat the *mascarpone* with the egg yolks, sugar, and vanilla until smooth. In a separate bowl, beat the egg whites with the sea salt until they form soft peaks. Gently fold the egg whites into the cream.

To assemble the *tiramisu*: Cover the bottom of 4 small glasses with coarsely crumbled ladyfingers. Add a layer of raspberry sauce to each and then one of *mascarpone* cream. Refrigerate for a few hours, or overnight, which is even better, as the ladyfingers will absorb the raspberry sauce. When ready to serve, dust with confectioners' sugar and top with the crumble, chopped pistachios, and add a few fresh raspberries.

Hazelnut chocolate molten cakes

with fleur de sel

A spoonful scooped out of a molten chocolate cake reveals a gooey center that's irresistible. These cakes are for chocolate lovers, and if you're like me, you'll always leave room for one. My recipe combines dark chocolate and hazelnut-flavored chocolate, and the cakes are served in individual molds so each person can enjoy his or her own little dish. When friends are with us for dinner, I like to prepare the cakes at the last minute with all of us gathered in the kitchen, chatting away and waiting for the magic to happen in the oven. It's worth the short wait!

Preheat the oven to 450°F (230°C). Butter the ramekins, then coat them with flour and tap the excess out. Melt the dark chocolate and butter in a bain-marie (see Basic Cooking Techniques, page 27, for instructions).

In the bowl of a stand mixer, combine the eggs with the sugar and *fleur de sel* and beat until the batter has tripled in volume and is light and pale in color; this will take about 8 minutes. Add the vanilla and fold in the flour, then the melted chocolate-butter mixture, making sure to keep the batter light each time.

Divide three-quarters of the batter among the ramekins and add one piece of hazelnut chocolate at the center of each mold. Cover with the rest of the batter. At this point, if you want, you can refrigerate the cakes until you are ready to bake and serve them. If you do, bring them back to room temperature before baking.

Place the cakes in the oven and bake for 10 to 12 minutes (if you bake 6 cakes, they tend to need 10 minutes only); remember that the less time you bake the cakes, the more gooey the inside will be. Remove from the oven and leave them to rest for 5 minutes. Flip them swiftly onto dessert plates or serve them directly in the ramekins. Dust with confectioners' sugar and serve. A scoop of whipped cream or ice cream served with the cakes is a nice touch too.

Makes 4 to 6 cakes, depending on the size

You will need: four ¾-cup ramekins or six ⅔-cup ramekins

6 tablespoons (85 g; 3 oz) unsalted butter, plus more for the molds
Flour of your choice, to dust the molds
4 oz (115 g) dark chocolate (70% cocoa)
2 large eggs plus 1 egg yolk
¼ cup (50 g; 1 ¾ oz) blond cane sugar
½ teaspoon *fleur de sel*
1 teaspoon pure vanilla extract
3 tablespoons (22 ½ g; ¾ oz) hazelnut or millet flour
1 oz (30 g) hazelnut-flavored chocolate, cut into 4 pieces
Confectioners' sugar, to dust

Index